A Gnostic Prayerbook

Rites, Rituals, Prayers and Devotions
for Independent Gnostics

TABLE OF CONTENTS

Introduction   i

PRAYERBOOK

The Sign of the Cross	2
The Christos' Prayer	3
The Stranger's Prayer	4
Prayer to the Mother Barbelo	5
Prayers Upon Waking	6
Prayers Upon Retiring	7
Prayer Before A Meal	8
Prayer of Protection Invoking the Four Lights	9
Litany Against Fear Invoking the Four Lights	10
Prayer for Protection of a House	11
Prayer for the Sick	12
Amulet for the Sick	13
Prayer of Blessing a Person	14
Prayer for the Well-Being of a Child	15
Prayer for Travelers	16
Prayer for Divine Guidance	17
Prayer for Comfort in Troubled Times	18
Prayer for the Neglected	19
Prayer for the Poor in Spirit	20
Prayer for Victims of the Archons	21
Prayer for Our Enemies	22

Prayer for Peace   23

Prayer for a Deceased Person   24

Prayer for All the Deceased   25

Litany of Thanksgiving   26

General Thanksgiving   28

Thanksgiving for Gnosis   29

The Shepherd's Prayer   30

Prayer to the Christos from the Acts of John   31

Ode to Sophia from The Acts of Thomas   33

Prayer of the Apostle Paul   35

RITES AND RITUALS

Rites of Consecration   37

Eucharist: The Mystery of Communion   44

A Mystery Of Baptism   47

A Mystery Of The Chrism   55

Initiation: The Mystery Of The Five Seals   60

Sacrament of the Apple   72

Blessing Ritual for a House   79

Ritual of Self-healing and Laying-on of Hands   83

Sacrament of Reconciliation or Confession   89

Mysteries Of The Gnostic Ascent   91

Appendix 1: A Gnostic Chaplet   128

Appendix 2: The Recurrent Mysteries   130

Appendix 3. Rulers of the Body for Healing Rites   133

Introduction

This little prayerbook is intended for use by the independent Gnostic practitioner. The school of thought now known as "Gnostic," or "Sethian," left behind a number of pseudopigraphical texts, most substantially represented in the collection found at Nag Hammadi, Egypt in 1945. Other schools of thought represented in this book are the Valentinian, the Hermetic, the various pagan groups who compiled the Greek Magical Papyri, and, of course, the wide range of organized Christian bodies extant during this period. These groups provided the inspiration for the prayers and rituals included herein.

There are a lot of so-called modern "Gnostic" churches and organizations, but, if you're like me, you'll find much about them deeply unsatisfying, if not unsettling. There are a few exceptions to this rule; I am particularly fond of individuals in L'Eglise Gnostique and the Alpha and Omega Christian Gnostic Church. These guys (and gals) tend to have their heads on their shoulders, so to speak. They know on which side their spiritual bread is buttered. Get me?

Nonetheless, it can be difficult, for various reasons, to find and participate in any modern Gnostic organization, since so much of what is out there is unmitigated crap. In point of fact, you're truer to the spirit of the original Gnostic groups if you attend a mainstream Christian church and practice Gnostic prayer and ritual as a parallel.

Suffice to say that the Gnostic path is never popular, never dependent upon "special secrets" or fancy outfits, perfectly suited for independent practice if you're so inclined.

Or, if you're like me, you might just prefer to abide by the words of Christ in Matthew's Gospel:

But when you pray, go into your room, close the door and pray to your Father, who is unseen. Then your Father, who sees what is done in secret, will reward you. (Matt 6:6)

Look, I'm not sure why you're interested in this whole "Gnostic" thing anyhow, but one thing we can be certain of regarding the Gnostic groups is that they prayed. So, I cobbled together this little collection, and I'm now passing it along to you.

But hey, you might ask, or someone might ask of you, aren't some of these rites and rituals mighty "priesty"? Shouldn't I have some kind of special ordination or be part of an apostolic succession or something if I really want to do this stuff? Well **I** don't know. That's up to you, really. Personally, I'm not into the whole Apostolic Succession thing; personally, I think Apostolicity is something inherent within the community of believers. So basically, in my book, what you do with this stuff is up to you.

The prayers, rites, rituals and devotions in this book are based on those found in a number of sacred texts from various religious traditions which flourished in Europe, North Africa and West Asia during the First through Seventh Centuries CE. Some of the material herein has been published previously in *The Book of the Stranger* and *Mysteries of the Gnostic Ascent*. See also the list of sources in the back of this book. Material from/inspired by the Nag Hammadi Library will be marked "NHL," from the Greek Magical Papyri "PGM," etc.

For more information on the Gnostics and their era, we highly recommend *The Gnostics: Myth, Ritual, and Diversity in Early Christianity* by David Brakke. For more about the author's approach to the modern Gnostic practice, please see *This Way: Making Sense of Gnosis in a Nonsensical Reality* (ISBN: 1456539418).

General Considerations

Materials

The practitioner is encouraged to be as DIY with materials as possible. Homemade items are best; there's no need to dress up in traditional priestly garb or any such stuff-- no need to purchase fancy hats or expensive icons. Making your own aspergillum for sprinkling holy water can be pretty fun-- think watering cans, laundry sprinklers and shower heads.

Rubrics appear in the texts in italic. When the rubrics indicate the Sign of the Cross be made over a person or object, an equal-armed cross can be made with the right hand about six inches from the sternum, while the left hand touches the heart, the index and middle finger of the right hand extended at a ninety degree angle, and the other fingers folded under the hand.

Barbrous Names And Intonation

Untranslatable "words of power" have been left in these texts as they appear in the originals. Those uncomfortable with intonation of these words may omit them or replace them, though the effectiveness of including them, even if imperfectly pronounced, cannot be overstated.

Pronunciation should be syllabic; examples follow. Intonation can be internal or vocalized. A brief pronunciation guide will assist:

VOWELS

a: pronounced as in "**are**."
e: as in "h**e**h."
i: as in "s**ee**d."
o: as in "g**o**at."
u: as in "m**oo**n."

DIPHTHONGS

aa: pronounced as in "**aa**rdvark."
ae: as in "r**ay**."
ai: as in "st**ye**"
ao: as in "y**ow**."
au: as in "**au**bergine."

ea as in "ear."
ee: as in "pay Amy."
ei: as in "lei."
eo: as in "mayonaise."
eu: as in "eww."

ia as in "free apple."
ie: as in "mead."
io: as in "yo-yo."
iu: as in "pew."

oa as in "boa."
oe: as in "go ape."
oi: as in "oink."
oo: as in "go over."
ou: as in "slow ooze."

ua as in "water."
ue: as in "wave."
ui: as in "wee."
uo: as in "quote."

CONSONANTS

B: as in boy.
C: as in cold.
Ch: as in as German "ich."
D: as in dog.
G: as in girl.
H: as in hat.
J/Y: as in jerry.
K: as in king.
L: as in louse.
M: as in mouse.
N: as in net.
P: as in pick.
Ph: as in phone.
Ps: as in wasps.

R: as in rug.
S: as in snake.
T: as in tick.
Th: as in Thai, but slightly softer.
V: as in vase.
X: as in axe.
Z: as in dz

SOME EXAMPLES

Armozel: AR-mo-zel.
Oriael: OR-eeya-el.
Davethai: DA-veh-t(h)aye.
Eleleth: EH-leh-leht(t)h.
Christos: CHREES-tos.
Sophia: sof-EEYA.
Yesseus Mazareus Yessedekeus: JESS-ews ma-za-REH-ews
jesse-DEH-keh-ews.
IAO: EE-AH-OH.

PRAYERBOOK

The Sign of the Cross

touch Forehead: Nous (Mind),
touch Solar Plexus: Christos (Christ),
touch Shoulder: Pistis (Faith)
touch Shoulder: Sophia (Wisdom),
touch Heart: Amen.

The Christos' Prayer

Unknown Mystery who dwells above the Pleroma, we honor your holy names. May your Aeons unfold over the World, and may your work be accomplished within the World as it is accomplished in the Pleroma. Provide us with the nourishment we require, and forgive us our imperfections as we try to forgive those who do us harm. Help us achieve the gnosis of the Light, and keep us safe from the clutches of the Archon, now and forever. Amen.

The Stranger's Prayer

O Lord God,
You who are above all the great eternal realms,
You who have neither beginning nor end,
Bestow upon us a spirit of knowledge
For the revelation of your mysteries,
To come to a knowledge of ourselves:
Where we have come from,
Where we are going,
And what we should do in order to live. Amen.

Prayer to the Mother Barbelo

Holy Mother, You are the life within all. With you we share the fall into ignorance, and it is with you that we share the ascent into life and light. Resurrect us. Awaken us to our true selves. Initiate us into your mysteries-the mysteries of the Christos. Help us to see the spark in all who come across our path, and serve them as a spark of God. Amen

Prayers Upon Waking

1. Great Invisible Spirit, Triple-Powered One, Spirit of Light, be with me as I humbly undertake to glorify you in the World of Forms. Let each thought I think, each word I utter, each step I take and each action I commit testify to the gnosis of your grace and glory. ♦ Nous, Christos, Pistis Sophia, Amen.

2. O Most Holy Christos and Sophia, be with me and watch over me as I go about my day. I give thanks to you for another opportunity to serve others and in so doing serve you. ♦ Nous, Christos, Pistis Sophia, Amen.

3. Unknown Father and Glorious Barbelo, grant that this day is like that heavenly day which has no night, and like the perfect sun which never sets. In my heart, I strive to be this perfect day, and in me dwells the light which does not fail. ♦ Nous, Christos, Pistis Sophia, Amen.

Prayers Upon Retiring

1. Great Invisible Spirit, Triple-Powered One, Spirit of Light, thank you for the gifts you have given me today, especially.... Steady my feet, as they have stumbled from your Path throughout this day, and forgive me for missing the mark, especially.... Be with us through the darkness, and bless us even to the morn. ✦ Nous, Christos, Pistis Sophia, Amen.

2. O Most Holy Christos and Sophia, thank you for your presence and assistance which guided me throughout the day. Although I dwell within the realms of imperfection, your presence helps guide me and protect me from morning until night. Forgive my transgressions, and comfort me tonight as you comforted Jesus in the Garden of Gethsemane. ✦ Nous, Christos, Pistis Sophia, Amen.

3. Unknown Father and Glorious Barbelo, I pray for your protection and solace as I lay down to sleep this night. Protect me from the visions and nightmares of the Archon, and fill my night with restful sleep and dreams of your blessed realms. ✦ Nous, Christos, Pistis Sophia, Amen.

Prayer Before A Meal

Most Holy Christos and Sophia, we give thanks to you for the gifts you have given us and ask you to bless this meal; grant also that we may be mindful of those in need or trouble. ✠ Nous, Christos, Pistis Sophia, Amen.

Prayer of Protection
Invoking the Four Lights

In the names of the Most Holy Christos and Sophia. Before me Armozel, Behind me Davethai, to my Left, Oriel, to my Right Eleleth. O you Four Luminaries who are Light above all Lights, be with me and protect me from the workings of the Archons that beset me! ✢ Amen, Amen, Amen, Amen!

Litany Against Fear
Invoking the Four Lights

Sophia (Wisdom),
Eirini (Peace),
Phronesis (Perfection):
Eleleth.
Idea (Idea),
Agape (Love),
Synesis (Understanding):
Davethai.
Mneme (Memory),
Aisthesis (Perception),
Epinoia (Conception):
Oriel.
Morphos (Form),
Alitheia (Truth),
Charis (Grace):
Armozel. (Repeat as often as needed.)

Prayer for Protection of a House

In the name of the Unknown Father and the Glorious Mother Barbelo, I bind you, Archonic scorpion, 315 times. Preserve this house with its occupants from all evil, from all bewitchment of spirits of the air and human hand and eye and sickness and sting of scorpion and bite of snake, through the name of the highest God, Naias Meli, XUROURO AAAAAA BAINCHOOOCH MARIIIIIIL ENAG KORE. Be on guard, O lord, O son of David according to the flesh, the one born of the Holy Virgin Mary, O holy one, highest God, from the Holy Sophia. Glory to you, o heavenly king! ✠ Nous, Christos, Pistis Sophia, Amen. (PGM)

Prayer for the Sick

In the name of the Christos and Sophia. ✢ In the sheep-pool in Soloam — its name in Hebrew is Bethsaida — the lord was found , in the Portico of Solomon the master was found. He healed the person who was bedridden by means of the Logos, and he opened the blind man's eyes. Hence we also, along with the archangels and the bodiless Aeons, shout and call out and say, Holy is God, whom the Aeons praise and the Angels revere. Holy, mighty is he, whom the chorus of bodiless Aeons glorifies. Holy, immortal is he, who was revealed in the manger of the animals. Heal and make well the body of your servant N. ✢ Nous, Christos, Pistis Sophia, Amen. (ACM)

Amulet for the Sick

(To be inscribed on parchment and worn around the arm of the infirm)

Jesus Christ
heals
the chill
and the
fever
and every
disease of the
body of N., who wears
the amulet daily
and intermittently.
They are quick! Amen, Alleluia. ✝✝✝
             ✝   ✝   ✝
ERICHTHONIE
RICHTHONIE
ICHTHONIE
CHTHONIE
THONIE
ONIE
NIE
IE
E   Let the white wolf,

the white wolf,

the white wolf
heal the shivering
fever of N.
They are quick! ✝✝
(ACM)

Prayer of Blessing a Person

I invoke you, Almighty God, who is above every Ruler and Archon and Aeon and everything that has been named, who is enthroned above the Pleroma before you, through our Lord Jesus Christ and Lady Sophia, the beloved Mother and Child. Send out to N., Lord, your luminaries, who stand opposite your altar and are appointed for your holy services, Armozel, Oriel, Daveithai, Eleleth. Let them accompany N. today, during all hours of day and night, and grant N. victories, favor, good luck, success with all people small and great whom he/she may encounter today, during all hours of day and night. For N. has before him/Her Jesus Christ and Sophia, who attend him/her and accompany him/her; behind him/her Yao Sabaoth; on his/her right and left the God of Abraham, Isaac and Joseph; over his/her face and heart Armozel, Oriel, Davethai, Eleleth. Protect N. from every archon, male or female, and from every stratagem and from every name, for he/she is sheltered under the wings of Sophia. O Jesus Christ, king of all the Aeons, almighty, inexpressible one, nurturer, master, almighty, noble child, kindly son, unutterable and inexpressible name, true form, unseen forever and ever. ✛   Nous, Christos, Pistis Sophia, Amen.

Prayer for the Well-Being of a Child

Most Holy Unknown Father and Radiant Mother Barbelo, we stand in your presence to call upon your protection and grace for the benefit of this child, N. Let him/her grow and care for him/her. Prescribe what is good. Fill him/her with understanding and the knowledge of Sophia. Open the organs of perception of his/her heart, that he/she may know only good things. Let people rejoice over his/her growth. Entrust him to the sheepfold of the Christos. For you are the preexistent Lord who has made us into your image and likeness. Take away all sickness and ill health from this child. Protect him/her against diseases of fever, against a chill, against evil wishes and influences, against harmful sicknesses — take them away from him/her. Grant him/her safety. For you are the Lord through whom the healing of all sickness comes, and you are the health of soul and body and spirit, through the favor and philanthropy of your son Jesus Christ, our lord, through whom be the glory to you and to him and the Holy Sophia, now and always, forever and ever.

✟   Nous, Christos, Pistis Sophia, Amen.

Prayer for Travelers

I used to command the Rhodian winds
And your regions of the sea
Whenever I'd want to set sail.
Whenever I'd want to stay there,
I'd say to the regions of the sea:
'Don't smite the sea with your blows;
Lay smooth the brine for seafarers.'
Then every fair wind is raised;
They shut out the blasts, and so, Christos and Sophia, grant
The impassible to be passable.
✠ Nous, Christos, Pistis Sophia, Amen. (PGM)

Prayer for Divine Guidance

Holy Sophia, grant me your Divine Wisdom and guidance. Shed your light on the path before me and keep me from stumbling. Guide my feet as you guided the feet of the Aeons who ascended and descended the shining ladder of Jacob, and lead me to the best and finest Path of gnosis. ✟ Nous, Christos, Pistis Sophia, Amen.

Prayer for Comfort in Troubled Times

Holy Comforter, Blessed Lady, surround your servant N. with a loving blanket of warmth. Make still his/her sorrow and grant him/her a restful peace in this time of trial. Bless him/her and be with him/her always. ✢ Nous, Christos, Pistis Sophia, Amen.

Prayer for the Neglected

Most Holy Logos, stretch out your hands to all of your charges and lift them as you lifted the sinful woman, especially those who have received no thought or mention in prayer or service, who are neglected and unloved in body, mind, or spirit within this World. Open the doors to the hearts of the glorious Aeons for those who have been cast away in this World of Forms. ✝   Nous, Christos, Pistis Sophia, Amen.

Prayer for the Poor in Spirit

Dearest Sophia, we pray that you may rekindle the divine spark within all your poor children of the Light, that the Logos may lift them into the limitless joy and brilliance of the Pleroma. ☦Nous, Christos, Pistis Sophia, Amen.

Prayer for Victims of the Archons

Great Invisible Spirit and Holy Mother Barbelo, extend your
loving Word and Wisdom into the Black Iron Prison. Rescue
your children who have been led astray or otherwise injured
by the deceptions of the Rulers of This World. Grant the
infinite compassion of the Pleroma to all who have been
ensnared by the Works and Deeds of Falsehood, that we may
not take error too seriously. ✢Nous, Christos, Pistis Sophia,
Amen.

Prayer for Our Enemies

Dearest Christos, who has instructed us to love those who work against us, so do we pray for love and compassion for them. May all those who hate, those who are violence, those who are blinded by prejudice, those who see others as though these others are undeserving of your love be brought into the fold of goodness and light. May their errors be forgiven and their actions become loving and kind, and may they come to join the community of Knowers that they may experience the gnosis of the Limitless Light. ✟Nous, Christos, Pistis Sophia, Amen.

Prayer for Peace

Great Invisible Spirit and Holy Mother Barbelo, extend your loving Word and Wisdom into the Black Iron Prison and establish a peacable dominion in all of the Nations of the Earth. Demolish the illusions of the Archons which divide your children and turn us against one another, and bring us together under the banner of unity and love. ✢Nous, Christos, Pistis Sophia, Amen.

Prayer for a Deceased Person

Immortal and everlasting Christos and Glorious Mother
Sophia, guide the spirit of N. through the manifest regions of
the Air that he/she may ascend through the realms of the
Aeons and take his/her rightful place in the Pleroma. ⊕Nous,
Christos, Pistis Sophia, Amen.

Prayer for All the Deceased

Great Invisible Spirit and Holy Mother Barbelo, guide and watch over the spirits of all those who have departed from this World of Forms, and establish them in the communities of the realms of unity and perfection. ✢Nous, Christos, Pistis Sophia, Amen.

Litany of Thanksgiving

Let us give Thanks to the Unknown Father and Glorious Mother Barbelo for the many gifts they have graciously bestowed upon us.

For the perfection of the Pleroma,

I thank you.

For the presence of the Christos and the Most Holy Sophia within this imperfect world,

I thank you.

For the wisdom of those from whom we have learned of gnosis,

I thank you.

For those who have achieved gnosis,

I thank you.

For those who have not yet achieved gnosis,

I thank you.

For the limitless opportunities to serve our fellows,

I thank you.

For those who have given us service,

I thank you.

For those who are ignorant of the Word,

I thank you.

For those who work against us,

I thank you.

For all of the moments of love and beauty within this imperfect world,

I thank you.

For health of body and mind,

I thank you.

For all of the gifts of experience which you have made manifest in our lives,

I thank you.

Glory be to the Christos and Sophia, and to the Unknown Father and Glorious Mother Forever and Ever. Amen.

General Thanksgiving

Dearest Father, most Gracious Mother Barbelo, thank you for this wonderful gift which you have given, and grant us the mindfulness to appreciate it and return it to others. ✟Nous, Christos, Pistis Sophia, Amen.

Thanksgiving for Gnosis

O Most Holy Father and Radiant Mother Barbelo, we give thanks to You! Every soul and heart is lifted up to You, undisturbed name, honored with the name 'God' and praised with the name 'Barbelo,' for to everyone and everything comes your kindness and affection and love, and any teaching there may be that is sweet and plain, giving us mind, speech, and gnosis: mind, so that we may understand You, speech, so that we may expound You, gnosis, so that we may know You. We rejoice, having been illuminated by Your knowledge. We rejoice because You have shown us Yourself. We rejoice because while we were in the body, You have made us divine through Your knowledge.

The thanksgiving of the one who attains to You is one thing: that we know You. We have known You, intellectual light. Life of life, we have known You. Womb of every creature, we have known You. Womb pregnant with the nature of the Father, we have known You. Eternal permanence of the begetting Father, thus have we worshiped Your goodness. There is one petition that we ask: we would be preserved in knowledge. And there is one protection that we desire: that we not stumble in this kind of life. Amen. (NHL)

The Shepherd's Prayer

Holy are You, O God, the Father of the Universe.

Holy are You, O God, whose Will perfects itself by means of its own Powers.

Holy are You, O God, who wills to be known and are known by Your own.

Holy are You, who did by Logos make to consist the things that are.

Holy are You, of whom all Nature has been made an image.

Holy are You, whose Form Nature has never made.

Holy are You, more powerful than all power.

Holy are You, transcending all pre-eminence.

Holy are You, better than all praise.

Accept my reason's offerings, from soul and heart stretched up to You, O You unutterable, unspeakable, Whose Name none but the Silence can express.

Give ear to me who pray that I may never of Gnosis fail, which is our common being's nature; and fill me with Your Power, and with this Grace, that I may give the Light to those in ignorance.

For this cause I believe, and I bear witness; I go to Life and Light. Blessed are You, O Father. Your offspring would holy be as You are holy, even as You gave Your full authority. Nous, Christos, Pistis Sophia, Amen. (CH)

Prayer to the Christos from the *Acts of John*

What praise, what offering, what thanksgiving, shall we, in breaking bread, speak of but you alone? We glorify Your Name which has been spoken by the Father; we glorify Your Name which has been spoken through the Son; we glorify the Resurrection shown to us through You; we glorify Your Seed, Word, Grace, Faith, Salt, True Pearl, Treasure, Plough, Greatness, Net, and Diadem, Him who has been called for our sakes the Son of Man, Truth, Rest, and Gnosis, Power, Law, Frankness, Hope, Love, Freedom, and Going-for-refuge to You. For You alone are one Lord, the Root of Deathlessness, and Source of Incorruptibility, Seat of the Æons. All these have You been called for us, that we invoking you by them, may know that as we are we never can embrace Your Greatness, greatness that can alone be contemplated by the Pure, for it is imaged in Your person alone. Amen. (NTA)

Ode to Sophia from the *Acts of Thomas*

The Maiden is Light's daughter; the King's radiance is treasured in her. She reigns majestic and delightful; she shines in radiant beauty.

Her garments are like spring flowers; the fragrance of sweet odors streams from them. The King sits above her head enthroned, with immortal food feeding immortals at his table.

Truth crowns her head; Joy plays at her feet. When she opens her mouth all psalms of praise stream forth.

Thirty-two sing praises to her. Her tongue is like the entrance veil, only moved by those who enter.

Her neck towers like a ladder; the first creator built it. Her hands resemble the band of Æons, proclaiming them; her fingers point toward the City's Gates.

Light streams from her bridal chamber, which pours forth the fragrance of balsam and sweet herbs, delicious scents of myrrh and savoury; with myrtle wreaths and masses of sweet flowers strewn within. Her bridal bed is decked with garlands.

Her bridesmen group around her; they are seven in number and she picked them herself. Seven, too, are her bridesmaids, dancing before her.

Twelve serve and attend her; their eyes always look for the Bridegroom, that He might fill them with light.

They will be in joy everlasting with Him; and will take their seats at that feast where the Great Ones assemble, and remain at that banquet of which the Eternal alone are deemed worthy.

They shall be clad in kingly dress, and put on robes of light, and both shall exult in joy and bliss, singing praise to the Father.

For they have received His glorious radiance; and when they see Him, their Lord, they are filled with light. They have received immortal food from Him, immortal.

They've drunk wine that slakes men's thirst forever, nor suffer fleshly desire. So with the Living Spirit they glorify Truth's Father, and sing their praise to Wisdom's Mother. (NTA)

Prayer of the Apostle Paul

O Lord of Lords, show me your light, give me your mercy! My Redeemer, redeem me, for I am yours; the one who has come forth from you. You are my mind; bring me forth! You are my treasure house; open for me! You are my fullness; take me to you! You are (my) repose; give me the perfect thing that cannot be grasped!

I invoke you, the one who is and who pre-existed in the name which is exalted above every name, through Jesus Christ, the Lord of Lords, the King of the ages; give me your gifts, of which you do not repent, through the Son of Man, the Spirit, the Paraclete of truth. Give me authority when I ask you; give healing for my body when I ask you through the Evangelist, and redeem my eternal light soul and my spirit. And the First-born of the Pleroma of grace -- reveal him to my mind!

Grant what no angel eye has seen and no archon ear (has) heard, and what has not entered into the human heart which came to be angelic and (modeled) after the image of the psychic God when it was formed in the beginning, since I have faith and hope. And place upon me your beloved, elect, and blessed greatness, the First-born, the First-begotten, and the wonderful mystery of your house; for yours is the power and the glory and the praise and the greatness for ever and ever. Amen. (NHL)

RITES AND RITUALS

Rites of Consecration

For use in various rituals and blessings.

Consecration of Salt

Let us pray.

Make the sign of the cross in the salt.

Nous, Christos, Pistis, Sophia, Amen.

The apostles said, "May our entire offering obtain salt." They called Sophia "salt". Without it, no offering is acceptable. But Sophia is barren, without child. For this reason, she is called "a trace of salt". (NHL)

Breathe onto the salt.

Almighty Father and All Encompassing Barbelo, we ask you to bless this creature of salt, as once you blessed the salt scattered over the water by the prophet Elisha. Wherever this salt is sprinkled, drive away the power of the Archon, and protect us always by the presence of Holy Sophia. Amen

Consecration of Ashes

Ashes may be obtained from charcoal and incense used in ritual (the best are frankincense, myrrh or sandlewood) or burned branches used on Palm Sunday.

Let us pray.

Make the sign of the cross in the ashes.

Nous, Christos, Pistis, Sophia, Amen.

The Christos said, "The person who is near me is near the fire. And the person who is far from me is far from the kingdom." (NHL)

Breathe onto the ashes.

Holy, Holy, Holy Christos, bless this creature of ash and cleanse it of all impurities that it may purify and sanctify that which it rests upon, as the corpse-world is redeemed through the purifying fire of the Pleroma which burns away the iniquities of the Archon. Amen.

Consecration of Water

Let us pray.

Make the sign of the cross over the water.

Nous, Christos, Pistis, Sophia, Amen.

Sprinkle a portion of consecrated salt into the water.

Come, you waters from the living waters, that were sent to us, the true from the true, the rest that was sent to us from the rest, the power of salvation that comes from that power which conquers all things and subdues them to its own will: come and dwell in these waters, that the gift of the Christos and Sophia may be perfectly consummated in them. Amen. (NTA)

Breathe over the water in the shape of a cross.

In the name of Yesseus Mazareus Yessedekeus, the living water and in the names of Micheus and Michar and Mnesinous, who preside over the spring of truth I ask the Holy Mother Sophia to bless this water. Amen.

Consecration of Oil

This oil is "multi-use." The best kind of oil is olive oil mixed with a small amount of balsam or hyssop.

Let us pray.

Make the sign of the cross in the oil.

Nous, Christos, Pistis, Sophia, Amen.

Sprinkle a portion of consecrated salt into the oil.

Holy oil, given to us for sanctification and anointment, sccret mystery through which the cross was shown to us, you are the straightener of crooked limbs, you are the softener of hard things, you show the hidden treasures, you are the sprout of goodness; let your power come. (NTA)

Breathe onto the oil.

Almighty Father and radiant Mother, bless this creature of oil so that those who share in its anointing may partake of the luminous light of the Pleroma. Let its holy power live and breathe in all that it rests upon. Let it make holy through its anointment, as the ministrations of the Christos make holy and sanctify the imperfections of the World of Forms. Amen.

General Prayer of Consecration of an Item

Let us pray.

Make the sign of the cross over the item.

Nous, Christos, Pistis, Sophia, Amen.

Mark the item with consecrated oil with the image of a circle, an equal armed cross, and a cross within a circle.

By these signs and in the name of the Christos and Sophia, I consecrate this [ITEM]. Let this [ITEM] be purified and blessed and consecrated that through it and by it the gnosis of the Limitless Light may further manifest within the World of Forms. Amen.

Consecration of a Room, Altar or Sacred Space

Let us pray.

Light incense and sprinkle holy water in four directions.
    (Facing East)   Harmozel-Orneos-Euthrounios
    (Facing North) Oraiael-Aphreudasos-Armedos- Arros
    (Facing West) Daveithe-Laraneus-Epiphanios-Eideos
    (Facing South) Eleleth-Kodere-Epiphanios-Allogenios

In the name of the Nous, the Christos, and Pistis Sophia. O you luminaries, surround and protect this sacred [Room/Altar/Space] that it may be used in service to the Christos and Sophia. In the name of the Christos and Sophia, I sanctify and bless this [Room/Altar/Space] in their service and to further the aims of the Pleroma. Amen.

Consecration of a Grave

Let us pray.

Make the sign of the cross over the grave.

Nous, Christos, Pistis, Sophia, Amen.

Sprinkle the grave with consecrated water and salt.

In the name of the Christos and Sophia, through whose benevolent presence the body of Jesus was laid to rest in the tomb, let the soul and spirit of the body which (rests/will rest) here come to know the refreshment and peace of eternal life within the repose of the Pleroma. Amen.

Eucharist: The Mystery of Communion

The Eucharist is best performed with home-baked bread and wine. The rite given here embraces the simplicity of the original event; it could certainly be extended if so desired. The practitioner is encouraged to share this service with others.

The Eucharist is the celebration of Thanksgiving after the fashion of Jesus Christ and his Apostles, during his last meal. This celebration also has rich and ancient roots, and may be celebrated outside of its Christological milieu should the Gnostic feel so called. Both performance of, and participation in the celebration of the Eucharist is radically open.

Before starting the service, the bread and wine should be prepared at the table, such that no unwrapping or uncorking is necessary at the service.

The wine should be poured out of the bottle into a jug (where it may be poured into a chalice), or into a bowl (into which the chalice may be dipped).

This simple ceremony may be incorporated into an ordinary meal, in which case, the wine and bread for the Eucharist should not be eaten or drunk until the Gnostic has administered them.

✜Nous, Christos, Pistis Sophia, Amen.

(Hands above the bread and wine in blessing:) Come highest Gift, Perfect Mercy, come. You knower of the Chosen's mysteries, descend. You who shares in all noble striver's struggles, come!

Come Silence, Revealer of the mighty of all the Greatness; come You who reveals that which is hidden, and uncovers all secrets!

Come Holy Dove, mother of two young twins; come Hidden Mother, revealed in deeds alone!

Come You who gives joy to all who are at one with You; come and commune with us in this thanksgiving eucharist which we are making in Your name, in this agapē to which we have assembled at Your call! (NTA)

Take bread and make sign of the cross in blessing over it.

"Now when the even was come he sat down with the twelve. and as they were eating, Jesus took bread, and blessed it,

Break the bread in half. If others are present, pass it to the persons on your left and right,

"and brake it, and gave it to his disciples, and said 'Take, eat; this is my body.

Dip the chalice in the wine, or fill it from the jug.

"And he took the cup, and gave thanks, and gave it to them, saying, Drink ye all of it; For this is my blood of the new testament, which is shed for many for the forgiveness of sins.

Breathe over the chalice in the shape of a cross. If others are present, pass the cup to the person on your right. When the bread and the wine return to you, you also eat and drink.

Now that we have partaken in the Mystery of the Eucharist, let us give thanks to the Limitless Light for the manifestation of the Fullness within this world of Limitations.

We give thanks to you, O Triple-Powered One, who, through the mediation of the Most Holy Christos and Sophia have manifested the Glory of the Pleroma. We pray for the continued unfolding of the Fullness within the world of imperfection, and thank you for the blessed gifts which we have received.

Unknown Mystery who dwells above the Pleroma, we honor your holy names. May your Aeons unfold over the World, and may your work be accomplished within the World as it is accomplished in the Pleroma. Provide us with the nourishment we require, and forgive us our imperfections as we try to forgive those who do us harm. Help us achieve the gnosis of the Light, and keep us safe from the clutches of the Archon, now and forever. ✠Nous, Christos, Pistis Sophia, Amen.

The rite concluded, all present wish peace to one another.

A Mystery Of Baptism

The Baptism may be performed as a head-washing, a sprinkling or a total immersion, depending upon the desire of the catechumen. The sacrament of Baptism may be performed during another service.

Materials required: Baptismal aspergillum, font or tub (unless ceremony is being performed in a river).

The catechumen should be dressed in clean garments, preferably of white. The catechumen may choose for him or herself a baptismal name to signify rebirth in the Christos and Sophia.

✠Nous, Christos, Pistis Sophia, Amen.

It is the will of God the Father and of Barbelo the Mother that we should be redeemed from the World of Imperfections through faith in, and knowledge of our most Holy Saviour. That we may come to know the Fullness of the Pleroma, the Lord has ordained the Mystery of Baptism by Water, that we may be reborn and receive the resurrection while still living. On this day, I stand ready to receive this Mystery.

Hear me as I sing praises to you, o Mystery who existed before every Aeon.

You are the Light which is brighter than all Lights,
You are the Height which is higher than all Heights.
The Living Animals ran from you, and to you shall the Living Animals return.

All things have emanated from you, and to your bosom shall
all things withdraw.
I thank you, who is beyond all Thanks.
I give praise to you, who is beyond all Praise.
I love you, who is the source of all Love.
Shed your glory upon me.
Amen.

As a symbol of my dedication to the gnosis of the Limitless
Light, I take upon myself and my spirit the name N.

I stand before the Christos and Sophia as a seeker of Gnosis,
which offers me redemption from the World of Forms. I will
seek to come to know myself, for, "he who has not known
himself has known nothing, but he who has known himself
has at the same time already achieved gnosis about the depth
of the all." (NHL)

*Make the Sign of the Cross on your crown, forehead, mouth and
heart.*

I receive the Seal of the Cross on my crown, forehead, mouth
and heart. By this sign shall I be known from this day
forward.

Let us listen to the words of Valentinus concerning the
sacrament of baptism:

> As for the baptism which exists in the fullest sense, into
> which the Totalities will descend and in which they
> will be, there is no other baptism apart from this one
> alone, which is the redemption into God, Father, Son
> and Holy Spirit, when confession is made through faith
> in those names, which are a single name of the gospel,
> when they have come to believe what has been said to
> them, namely that they exist.

From this they have their salvation, those who have believed that they exist. This is attaining in an invisible way to the Father, Son, and Holy Spirit in an undoubting faith. And when they have borne witness to them, it is also with a firm hope that they attained them, so that the return to them might become the perfection of those who have believed in them and (so that) the Father might be one with them, the Father, the God, whom they have confessed in faith and who gave (them) their union with him in knowledge.

The baptism which we previously mentioned is called "garment of those who do not strip themselves of it," for those who will put it on and those who have received redemption wear it. It is also called "the confirmation of the truth which has no fall." In an unwavering and immovable way it grasps those who have received the restoration while they grasp it. Baptism is called "silence" because of the quiet and the tranquility. It is also called "bridal chamber" because of the agreement and the indivisible state of those who know they have known him. It is also called "the light which does not set and is without flame," since it does not give light, but those who have worn it are made into light. They are the ones whom he wore.

Baptism is also called "the eternal life," which is immortality; and it is called "that which is, entirely, simply, in the proper sense, what is pleasing, inseparably and irremovably and faultlessly and imperturbably, for the one who exists for those who have received a beginning."

For, what else is there to name it apart from "God," since it is the Totalities, that is, even if it is given numberless names, they are spoken simply as a reference to it.

Just as he transcends every word, and he transcends every voice, and he transcends every mind, and he transcends everything, and he transcends every silence, so it is with those who are that which he is.

This is that which they find it to be, ineffably and inconceivably in its visage, for the coming into being in those who know, through him whom they have comprehended, who is the one to whom they gave glory. (NHL)

I, N., would be baptized (op: in the presence of those here assembled) in the name of the Father, and of the Son, and of the Holy Spirit.

I renounce the Archon, his works and his deeds.

I will live my life to the best of my ability, seeking gnosis wherever it may be found.

I state again: I will be baptized (op: in the presence of those here assembled) in the name of the Father, and of the Son, and of the Holy Spirit.

Stand before the water that will be used for the baptism.

By perfecting the water of baptism, Jesus emptied it of death. Thus we do go down into the water, but we do not go down into death, in order that we may not be poured out into the spirit of the world. When that spirit blows, it brings the winter. When the Holy Spirit breathes, the summer comes. (NHL)

Breathe upon the water in the sign of a cross.

In the name of Yesseus Mazareus Yessedekeus, the living water.
Breathe upon the water in the sign of a cross.

In the names of Micheus and Michar and Mnesinous, who preside over the spring of truth.

Breathe upon the water in the sign of a cross.

In the name of Sesengenpharanges, who presides over the baptism of the living.

So do I ask the Holy Mother Sophia to bless this water that through it the Living Water will wash away my imperfections so that I will be reborn in the light of gnosis.

Kneel, hands together as in prayer.

I state for the third time: I, N., would be baptized (op: in the presence of those here assembled) in the name of the Father, and of the Son, and of the Holy Spirit.

Place your arms in the form of a circle, hands still together.

This baptism is remission of sins: this brings forth light that is shed around us: this brings rebirth: this restores understandings: this mingles the spirit: this raises up a new person and makes him/her a partaker of the remission of sins. Glory be to you, hidden one, that are communicated in baptism. Glory to you, unseen power that is in baptism. Glory to you, renewal, whereby those that are baptized are renewed, and with affection take hold upon you. (NTA)

Sprinkle/wash/immerse in the water.

In the name of the Father, the Son, and the Holy Spirit, and in the name of the Limitless Light, the Father, Barbelo, the Christos and Sophia, so do I wash myself of the Life of the World of Forms.

> IE ieus EO ou EO Oua! Amen, Amen O Yesseus Mazareus Yessedekeus, O living water, O child of the child, O glorious name! Amen, Amen, aiOn o On, iiii EEEE eeee oooo uuuu OOOO aaaaa. Amen Amen, Ei aaaa OOOO, O existing one who sees the aeons! Amen, Amen, aee EEE iiii uuuuuu OOOOOOOO, who is eternally eternal! Amen, amen, iEa aiO, in the heart, who exists, u aei eis aei, ei o ei, ei os ei.

Place a white stole or scarf around your neck.

> This great name of yours is upon me, O self-begotten Perfect one, who is not outside me. I see you, O you who are visible to everyone. For who will be able to comprehend you in another tongue? Now that I have known you, I have mixed myself with the immutable.

I have armed myself with an armor of light; I have become light! For the Mother was at that place because of the splendid beauty of grace. Therefore, I have stretched out my hands while they were folded. I was shaped in the circle of the riches of the light which is in my bosom, which gives shape to the many begotten ones in the light into which no complaint reaches.

I shall declare your glory truly, for I have comprehended you, sou iEs ide aeiO aeie ois, O aeon, aeon, O God of silence! I honor you completely. You are my place of rest, O Son Es Es o e, the formless one who exists in the formless ones, who exists raising up the man in whom you will purify me into your life, according to your imperishable name. Therefore, the incense of life is in me.

I mixed it with water after the model of all archons, in order that I may live with you in the peace of the saints, you who exist really truly forever. (NHL)

Rise, hands still in prayer.

Now shall I walk, alive in the lands of the dead. I shall speak concerning the truth to those who seek it and of knowledge to those who, in their error, have committed sin. I shall make sure-footed those who stumble and stretch forth my hands to the sick. I shall nourish the hungry and set at ease those who are troubled. I shall foster those who love. I shall raise up and awaken those who sleep. (NHL)

Light baptismal candle.

Let the light of this candle remind me of the spark of light which lives in me, through which the Logos and the Holy Sophia manifest the goodness and perfection of the Pleroma. May the light of my gnosis shine ever brightly.

Unknown Mystery who dwells above the Pleroma, we honor your holy names. May your Aeons unfold over the World, and may your work be accomplished within the World as it is accomplished in the Pleroma. Provide us with the nourishment we require, and forgive us our imperfections as we try to forgive those who do us harm. Help us achieve the gnosis of the Light, and keep us safe from the clutches of the Archon, now and forever. ✠Nous, Christos, Pistis Sophia, Amen.

A Mystery Of The Chrism

The anointing shall be performed using consecrated olive oil. As says the Gospel of Philip, *"... It is from the olive tree that we got the chrism, and from the chrism, the resurrection."*

Materials necessary: "Cross of Light"-- a cross, preferably even-armed, fashioned of some kind of reflective material-- glass, plastic or metal; Consecrated Oil.

✢Nous, Christos, Pistis Sophia, Amen.

Most Holy Christos and Sophia, who did descend into the limitations of the World of Forms, be with me and watch over me this day, as I celebrate the transmission of the plasmate into my members and the awakening of the living information according to your presence. Amen.

A reading from the Gospel According to Philip:

> The chrism is superior to baptism, for it is from the word "Chrism" that we have been called "Christians," certainly not because of the word "baptism". And it is because of the chrism that "the Christ" has his name. For the Father anointed the Son, and the Son anointed the apostles, and the apostles anointed us. He who has been anointed possesses everything. He possesses the resurrection, the light, the cross, the Holy Spirit. (NHL)

I, N., now stand ready to accept the indwelling plasmate, the living information which has been passed down since the first inbreaking of the Pleroma into the World of Forms.

I open my heart through the Compassion of the Holy Spirit as mediated by the Logos, that the plasmate may dwell within me as living information.

I open my mind through the Wisdom of the Holy Spirit as mediated by the Logos, that the plasmate may dwell within me as living information.

I reject the works of the World of Forms, which will fade away when the consumation of consumations takes place.

I pray to God the Father and Barbelo the Mother, that the plasmate may incarnate within my heart and mind, and that the Logos may come to dwell within me.

Kneel.

O Yesseus Mazareus Yessedekeus, Most Holy Logos, Word above all words, Mind above all Minds, cultivate your Garden within me, that the Plasmate may find my soil fertile and place roots within me. As you have manifested the Light of Gnosis to your servants who have faithfully and sincerely called out for you, let it also manifest to me. I ask this through the Christos and Sophia. Amen.

After a moment of silent prayer, stand.

Dip your right thumb into the chrism oil, making the sign of the cross with the chrism oil on the following parts of your body.

The seal in the name of the Christos open my eyes, that I may awaken into gnosis.

The seal in the name of the Christos open my ears, that I may hear the music of the Aeons.

The seal in the name of the Christos open my nostrils, that the fragrance of the Father manifests within me.

The seal in the name of the Christos open my mouth, that I proclaim the Gospel of Truth with honesty and compassion.

The seal in the name of the Christos upon my hands, that they may accomplish the work of the Christos and Sophia within the World of Forms.

The seal in the name of the Christos upon my heart, that it becomes filled to overflowing with the compassion of the Christos and Sophia.

The seal in the name of the Christos upon my back, that I may always be shielded against the machinations of the Archon.

The seal in the name of the Christos upon my feet, that I may walk in the Way of gnosis.

I awaken, in the name of the Christos, in whom I am sealed!

Amen, amen, amen.

Another moment of silent prayer, during which retrieve the Cross of Light. Then,

I am prepared to receive the Mystery of the Cross.

Raise the Cross of Light above your head.

Behold the Sign of the Logos! Thus saith the Lord:

This cross of light is sometimes called the word by me for your sakes, sometimes mind, sometimes Jesus, sometimes Christos, sometimes door, sometimes a way, sometimes bread, sometimes seed, sometimes resurrection, sometimes Son, sometimes Father, sometimes Spirit, sometimes life, sometimes truth, sometimes faith, sometimes grace. And by these names it is called by men: but that which it truly is, as conceived of in itself and as spoken of to you, it is the marking-off of all things, and the firm uplifting of things fixed out of things unstable, and the harmony of wisdom, and indeed wisdom in harmony. (NTA)

My mouth has been cleansed of dust. Taking this Cross of Light, I speak my first words as Homoplasmate.

At this time, speak or write extemporaneously, according to the Movement of the Plasmate and the awakening of the Living Information. When you have concluded, the Cross of Light is returned it to its resting place.

Amen, Amen, Amen.

Unknown Mystery who dwells above the Pleroma, we honor your holy names. May your Aeons unfold over the World, and may your work be accomplished within the World as it is accomplished in the Pleroma. Provide us with the nourishment we require, and forgive us our imperfections as we try to forgive those who do us harm. Help us achieve the gnosis of the Light, and keep us safe from the clutches of the Archon, now and forever. ✟Nous, Christos, Pistis Sophia, Amen.

Let those who received the transmission of the Living Information this day, and those who have received it before, dwell forever in the refreshment of the Pleroma.

Amen.

Glory, Glory, Glory to You,
O Iesus Christos Parakletos Sophia,
Who was sent to redeem us,
O you who descended into the world of forms,
You ineffable Word and Wisdom,
Forgive us our transgressions,
Free us from the chains of limitation,
And carry us to the Fullness of the Limitless Light.

In the name of the ✢Nous, Christos, Pistis Sophia, Amen.

Initiation: The Mystery Of The Five Seals

The Mystery of the Five Seals is a self-initiation into Sethian Gnostic mythology.

Necessary Supplies:

> *Consecrated Oil of Sealing: myrrh & olive oil*
> *Consecrated Water*
> *Consecrated bread/wine*
> *Incense/Coals*
> *Recording of the tone of Seven Vowels (EFGABCD), or instrument to play it on*
> *Outer garment*
> *White Stole or Robe, representing Robe of Glory*

(Making the Sign of the Cross) In the name of The Great Invisible Spirit, the Holy Mother-Father Barbelo, the Pigeradamas, the Four Luminaries, Holy Word and Wisdom and the Father Echamma Seth, we ask you to bless, consecrate and sanctify our community as we gather today to celebrate the Mystery of Mysteries and participate in the celebration of the Living Waters and Baptism in Light. Amen.

O Lord God,
You who are above all the great eternal realms,
You who have neither beginning nor end,
Bestow upon us a spirit of knowledge
For the revelation of your mysteries,
To come to a knowledge of ourselves:
Where we have come from,
Where we are going,

And what we should do in order to live. Amen.

I speak the words of our most blessed predecessor, Dositheos, and participate in the mystery.

Recite First Stela of Seth:

> I bless you, Father Geradamas, I, as your own Son, Emmacha Seth, whom you begot without begetting, as a blessing of our God; for I am your own Son. And you are my mind, O my Father. And I, I sowed and begot; but you have seen the majesties. You stood imperishable. I bless you, Father. Bless us, Father. It is because of you that we exist; it is because of God that you exist. Because of you I am with that very one. You are light, since you behold light. You revealed light. You are Mirotheas; you are my Mirotheos. I bless you as God; I bless your divinity. Great is the good Self-begotten who stood, the God who had already stood. You come in goodness; you appeared, and you revealed goodness. I shall utter your name, for you are a first name. You are unbegotten. You appeared in order that you might reveal the eternal ones. You are he who is. Therefore you revealed those who really are. You are he who is uttered by a voice, but by mind are you glorified, you who dominion everywhere. Therefore the perceptible world too knows you because of you and your seed. You are merciful.
>
> And you are from another race, and its place is over another race. And now you are from another race, and its place is over another race. You are from another race, for you are not similar.

And you are merciful, for you are eternal. And your place is over a race, for you caused all these to increase; and for the sake of my seed. For it is you who knows it, that its place is in begetting. But they are from other races, for they are not similar. But their place is over other races, for their place is in life. You are Mirotheos.

I bless his power which was given to me, who caused the malenesses that really are to become male three times, who caused the femalenesses that really are to become female three times; he who was divided into the pentad, the one who was given to us in triple power, the one who was begotten without begetting, the one who came from that which is elect; because of what is humble, he went forth from the midst.

You are a Father through a Father, a word from a command. I bless you, Thrice Male, for you didst unite all through them all, for you empowered us. You arisen from one; from one you gone forth; you come to one. You saved, you saved, you saved us, O crown-bearer, crown-giver! We bless you eternally. We bless you, once we have been saved, as the perfect individuals, perfect on account of you, those who became perfect with you who is complete, who completes, the one perfect through all these, who is similar everywhere.

Thrice Male, you stood. You already stood. You were divided everywhere. You continued being one. And those whom you willed, you saved. But you will to be saved all who are worthy.

You are Perfect! You are Perfect! You are Perfect! (NHL)

Having received the gnosis of the Holy Invisible Spirit, I freely and of my own volition seek to join the community of knowers, the Great Immovable and Immutable Lineage of Emmacha Seth.

In order to be found worthy of acceptance into the Mysteries of the Five Seals, I now divest myself of my robes of corruptibility and allow the Most Holy Christos and Sophia to bear witness to your errors. I now remove my corruptible garment and confess my errors to the Most Holy Christos and Sophia.

Remove your outer garment and kneel. At this point, you may confess any errors with which you feel weighted, aloud or silently. Then:

I have shed my corruptible robes and confessed my errors to the Most Holy Christos and Sophia, and stand ready to receive the Mysteries of the Five Seals.

The Five Seals are Five Trees in Paradise, Five Powers Before the Throne, Five Directions, Five Elements, Five Wellsprings and Five Spiritual Waters of Baptism.

Bless the oil of sealing.

In the name of Yesseus Mazareus Yessedekeus, the living water.

Breathe upon the oil in the sign of a cross.

In the names of Micheus and Michar and Mnesinous, who preside over the spring of truth.

Breathe upon the oil in the sign of a cross.

In the name of Sesengenpharanges, who presides over the baptism of the living.

So do I ask the Holy Emmacha Seth to bless this oil of sealing that through it the Living Water will wash away my imperfections so that I may be reborn in the light of gnosis.

Anoint yourself with the oil of sealing in the shape of an encircled cross, five times as follows:

Anointing the eyes:

In the name of Barbelo, the great Mother Father, in the name of the Christos and Sophia, in the name of the Holy Light Armozel and in the name of Emmacha Seth, I seal my eyes with the First Seal. Attend to the mystery.

Make the sign of the cross with an illumined candle before your eyes.

Anointing the ears:

In the name of Barbelo, the great Mother Father, in the name of the Christos and Sophia, in the name of the Holy Light Oroeial and in the name of Emmacha Seth, I seal my ears with the Second Seal. Attend to the mystery.

Play the tune of the Seven Holy Vowels, EFGABCD.

Anointing the nose:

In the name of Barbelo, the great Mother Father, in the name of the Christos and Sophia, in the name of the Holy Light Davethai and in the name of Emmacha Seth, I seal my nose with the Third Seal. Attend to the mystery.

Make the sign of the cross with the fragrance of myrrh under your nose.

Anointing the mouth:

In the name of Barbelo, the great Mother Father, in the name of the Christos and Sophia, in the name of the Holy Light Eleleth and in the name of Emmacha Seth, I seal my mouth with the Fourth Seal. Attend to the mystery.

Place a piece of Eucharistic bread soaked in wine in your mouth.

Anointing the hands:

In the name of Barbelo, the great Mother Father, in the name of the Christos and Sophia, in the name of all of the Luminaries and in the name of Emmacha Seth, I seal my hands with the Fifth Seal. Attend to the mystery.

Wash your hands in consecrated water.

At this point, lie on your back on the ground, arms wide open in the shape of a cross, totally exposed to the Kosmos. If unable to lie prone, you may be seated with arms open.

Having been divested of my worldly garments, I lie spiritually naked and exposed to the World of Forms and the Powers thereof. However, I have now received the Five Seals and the Mysteries thereof.

I therefore accept the gnosis of our Holy Mother Father Barbelo?

I now renounce the Archons while exposed to them, accepting the protection and the gnosis granted to all members of the line of Emmacha Seth.

I renounce Athoth, the sheep-faced, and his false goodness?

I renounce you, Athoth.

I renounce Eloaios, the donkey-faced, and his false providence.

I renounce you, Eloaios.

I renounce Astaphaios, the hyena-faced, and his false divinity.

I renounce you, Astaphaios.

I renounce Yao, the seven-headed serpent-faced, and his false lordship.

I renounce you, Yao.

I renounce Sabaoth, the dragon-faced, and his false kingdom.

I renounce you, Sabaoth.

I renounce Adonin, the ape-faced, and his false zeal.
I renounce you, Adonin.

I renounce Sabbataios, the fire-faced, and his false understanding.

I renounce you, Sabbataios.

I indeed renounce all unrepentant Powers, even unto the Demiurge Yaldabaoth himself, and all of his works.

I renounce you, Yaldabaoth, and all of your Works and Deeds.

Hear me, you Archons and Powers of the Kosmos! I have renounced your Works and Deeds and your power over me is no more! I have accepted my heritage as a child of Emmacha Seth and have been sealed with the Five Seals in the name of the Christos and Sophia and the Perfect Human Poimael!

Take a moment to contemplate in silence. Then:

From the *Holy Book of the Great Invisible Spirit*: But from now on, through the incorruptible man Poimael, and they who are worthy of (the) invocation, the renunciations of the five seals in the spring-baptism, these will know their receivers as they are instructed about them, and they will know them (or: be known) by them. These will by no means taste death. (NHL)

From the words of Dositheos.

Recite Second Stela of Seth:

> Great is the first aeon, male virginal Barbelo, the first glory of the invisible Father, she who is called "perfect".
>
> You have seen first the one who truly pre-exists because he is non-being. And from him and through him you have pre-existed eternally, the non-being from one indivisible, triple power, you a triple power, you a great monad from a pure monad, you an elect monad, the first shadow of the holy Father, light from light.

We bless you, Mother, producer of perfection, aeon-giver. You have seen the eternal ones because they are from a shadow. And you have become numerable. And you did find, you did continue being one; yet becoming numerable in division, you are three-fold. You are truly thrice, you female one of the male one. And you are from a shadow of him, you a Hidden One, you a world of understanding, knowing those of the one, that they are from a shadow. And these are yours in the heart.

For their sake you have empowered the eternal ones in being; you have empowered divinity in living; you have empowered knowledge in goodness; in blessedness you have empowered the shadows which pour from the one. You have empowered this one in gnosis; you have empowered another one in creation.

You have empowered him who is equal and him who is not equal, him who is similar and him who is not similar.
You have empowered in begetting, and provided forms in that which exists to others. You have empowered these. - He is that One Hidden in the heart. - And you have come forth to these and from these . You are divided among them. And you become a great male noetic First-Appearer.

Fatherly God, divine child, begetter of multiplicity according to a division of all who really are, you have appeared to them all in a word. And you possess them all without begetting and eternally indestructible on account of you.

Salvation has come to us; from you is salvation. You wisdom, you knowledge; you truthfulness. On account of you is life; from you is life. On account of you is mind; from you is mind. You are mind, you a world of truthfulness, you a triple power, you threefold. Truly you are thrice, the aeon of aeons. It is you only who sees purely the first eternal ones and the unbegotten ones.

But the first divisions are as you were divided. Unite us as you have been united. Teach us those things which you see. Empower us that we may be saved to eternal life. For we are each a shadow of you as you are a shadow of that first pre-existent one. Hear us first. We are eternal ones. Hear us as the perfect individuals. You are the aeon of aeons, the all-perfect one who is established.

You have heard! You have heard!
You have saved! You have saved!
We give thanks! We bless you always! We shall glorify you! (NHL)

I now arise a child of Emmacha Seth, and take the investiture of my heritage.

Stand. Drapes the clean stole/robe around your shoulders.

In this community of knowers, I shall be known as N. I now stand as a child of Seth and his immovable, immutable lineage.

Recite Third Stela of Seth:

We rejoice! We rejoice! We rejoice!

We have seen! We have seen! We have seen the really pre-existent one, that he really exists, that he is the first eternal one.

From the words of Dositheos. O Unconceived, from you are the eternal ones and the aeons, the all-perfect ones who are established, and the perfect individuals.

We bless you, non-being, existence which is before existences, first being which is before beings, Father of divinity and life, creator of mind, giver of good, giver of blessedness!

We all bless you, knower, in a glorifying blessing, because of whom all these are existent and perfect, who knows you, through you alone. For there is no one who is active before you. You are an only and living spirit. And you know one, for this one who belongs to you is on every side. We are not able to express him. For your light shines upon us.

Present a command to us to see you, so that we may be saved. Knowledge of you, it is the salvation of us all. Present a command! When you dost command, we have been saved! Truly we have been saved! We have seen you by mind! You are them all, for you dost save them all, he who was not saved, nor was he saved through them. For you, you commanded us.

You are one. You are one, just as there is one who will say to you: You are one, you are a single living spirit. How shall we give you a name? We do not have it, For you are the existence of them all. You are the life of them all. You are the mind of them all. For you are he in whom they all rejoice.

You commanded all these to be saved through your word, the glory who is before him, Hidden One, blessed Senaon, he who begat himself, Asineu(s), Mephneus, Optaon, Elemaon the great power, Emouniar, Nibareus, Kandephoros, Aphredon, Deiphaneus, you who are Armedon to me, power-begetter, Thalanatheus, Antitheus, you who exist within yourself, you who are before yourself - and after you no one entered into activity.

As what shall we bless you? We are not empowered. But we give thanks, as being humble toward you. For you commanded us, as he who is elect, to glorify you to the extent we are able. We bless you because we were saved. Always we glorify you. For this reason we shall glorify you, that we may be saved to eternal salvation. We have blessed you, for we are empowered. We have been saved, for you willed always, that we all do this.

We all did this. The One who will remember these and give glory always will become perfect among those who are perfect and impassable beyond all things. For they all bless these individually and together. And afterwards they shall be silent. And just as they were ordained, they ascend. After the silence, they descend from the third. They bless the second; after these the first. The way of ascent is the way of descent.

I know therefore, as one who lives, that I have attained. And I taught myself the infinite things. I marvel at the truth which is within me, and at the revelation. (NHL)

In the Name of the Great Triple-Powered Invisible One, the Dark and Silent Mother Barbelo, The Most Holy Christos and the Divine and Radiant Sophia, Amen, Amen, Amen. ☥

Sacrament of the Apple

This short sacrament was inspired by a dream. Required material apple(s), holy water/aspergillum, incense, knife, bell.

In the name of the Nous, the Christos, and Pistis Sophia. Amen.

Father, Father, Father of the light,
who possesses the incorruptions,
hear us just as you have taken pleasure in your holy child
Jesus Christ.
For he became for us an illuminator in the darkness.
Yes, hear us!
Hear us, Father, just as you heard your only-begotten son,
and received him,
and gave him rest from any imperfection.
You are the one whose power is perfect;
your armor, resplendent, is full of the light above all lights;
your living presence touches the Pleroma;
the Word saves the Cosmos through the repentance of
Sophia;
life has come into existence because of you.
You are the thinking and the entire serenity of the solitary.
Again: Hear us just as you heard your elect.
Through your sacrifice, these will enter;
through their good works, these have saved their souls from
these blind limbs,
so that they might exist eternally.
Amen.

(Ringing bell) Oh you Lumniaries, Lights before the Throne of the Aeons of Barbelo and the Limitless Light, be present with us as we participate in this sacrament. May this place be sanctified and protected from all Archonic influence, and be made holy by your eternal and enduring presence.

(Light incense and sprinkle holy water in four directions.)

    (Facing East)   Harmozel-Orneos-Euthrounios
    (Facing North) Oraiael-Aphreudasos-Armedos- Arros
    (Facing West)   Daveithe-Laraneus-Epiphanios-Eideos
    (Facing South) Eleleth-Kodere-Epiphanios-Allogenios

In the name of the Nous, the Christos, and Pistis Sophia. Amen.

(Kneeling.)

Glory, Glory, Glory to You,
O Iesus Christos Parakletos Sophia,
Who was sent to redeem us,
O you who descended into the world of forms,
You ineffable Word and Wisdom,
Forgive us our transgressions,
Free us from the chains of limitation,
And carry us to the Fullness of the Limitless Light.
Amen.

(Place the apple on altar. Raising hands above the apple, intone willfully)

Holy Sophia, be with us and sanctify us. Unveil the Pleroma to us, and allow us a vision of that Kingdom which is forever spreading out upon the Earth, but which we do not see. Come upon and into this fruit as you descended into the Fruit in the Garden of Eden, granting the gnosis of the Light to our Holy Mother Eve and Holy Father Adam.

> Then the female spiritual principle came in the snake, the instructor; and it taught them, saying, "What did he say to you? Was it, 'From every tree in the garden shall you eat; yet - from the tree of recognizing good and evil do not eat'?"

> The carnal woman said, "Not only did he say 'Do not eat', but even 'Do not touch it; for the day you eat from it, with death you are going to die.'"

> And the snake, the instructor, said, "Do not be afraid. With death you shall not die; for it was out of jealousy that he said this to you. For he knows that when you eat from it, your intellect will become sober and you will come to be like gods, recognizing the difference that obtains between evil men and good ones."

> And the carnal woman took from the tree and ate; and she gave to her husband as well as herself; and these beings that possessed only a soul, ate. And their imperfection became apparent in their lack of knowledge; and they recognized that they were naked of the spiritual element, and took fig leaves and bound them upon their loins. (NHL)

(Slice apple in half across the width, holding aloft the two halves exposing seeds.)

Behold his promise, and her sign to us and to our descendants.

(Take a bite of the apple. Pass apple to all present, each taking a bite and passing them along. Each participant also takes a bite of the apple. More apples may be used for larger congregations, but care should be taken that enough is made available for all who wish to partake.

After everyone has partaken, the remnants (core, seeds, stem) are returned to the altar. Take up the remnants, holding them aloft.)

Now have we partaken of the fruit of the Tree of the Gnosis of Good and Evil. May our words and actions always reflect our origin in the Light and our residence in the Pleroma. Let us rest a moment in the silence of our glorious Lady Sophia, and contemplate the role of the Christos in our hearts and minds.

(Moment of silence.)

In the name of the Nous, the Christos, and Pistis Sophia. Amen.

As our corporeal bodies shall return to the dust from which we were made, so shall the corpse of this apple become one with the body of the Earth.

(Set apple remnants aside for composting.)

Let us praise the Lord after the fashion of Solomon the Wise.

My heart was pruned and its flower appeared, then grace sprang up in it, and my heart produced fruits for the Lord.

For the Most High circumcised me by His Holy Spirit, then He uncovered my inward being towards Him, and filled me with His love.

And His circumcising became my salvation, and I ran in the Way, in His peace, in the way of truth.

From the beginning until the end I received His gnosis.

And I was established upon the rock of truth, where He had set me.

And speaking waters touched my lips from the fountain of the Lord generously.

And so I drank and became intoxicated, from the living water that does not die.

And my intoxication did not cause ignorance, but I abandoned vanity,

And turned toward the Most High, my God, and was enriched by His favors.

And I rejected the folly cast upon the earth, and stripped it off and cast it from me.

And the Lord renewed me with His garment, and possessed me by His light.

And from above He gave me immortal rest, and I became like the land that blossoms and rejoices in its fruits.

And the Lord is like the sun upon the face of the land.

My eyes were enlightened, and my face received the dew;

And my breath was refreshed by the pleasant fragrance of the Lord.

And He took me to His Paradise, wherein is the wealth of the Lord's pleasure.

I beheld blooming and fruit-bearing trees,
And self-grown was their crown.

Their branches were sprouting and their fruits were shining.
From an immortal land were their roots.

And a river of gladness was irrigating them, And round about them in the land of eternal life.

Then I worshipped the Lord because of His magnificence.

And I said, Blessed, O Lord, are they who are planted in Your land, and who have a place in Your Paradise;

And who grow in the growth of Your trees, and have passed from darkness into light.

Behold, all Your laborers are fair, they who work good works, and turn from wickedness to your pleasantness.

For the pungent odor of the trees is changed in Your land,

And everything becomes a remnant of Yourself. Blessed are the workers of Your waters, and eternal memorials of Your faithful servants.

Indeed, there is much room in Your Paradise. And there is nothing in it which is barren, but everything is filled with fruit.

Glory be to You, O God, the delight of Paradise for ever. Hallelujah.

Having thus partaken of the Fruit of the Tree of the Gnosis of Good and Evil, let us depart this place and spread the Light of the Divine Sophia wherever we may tread. O you Holy Luminaries who stand before the throne of the Limitless Light, we thank you for your presence at this sacrament and honor your Light. Be with us as we return to the realm of limitations and the World of Forms.

(Facing South) Eleleth-Kodere-Epiphanios-Allogenios
(Facing West) Daveithe-Laraneus-Epiphanios-Eideos
(Facing North) Oraiael-Aphreudasos-Armedos-Arros
(Facing East) Harmozel-Orneos-Euthrounios

In the name of the Nous, the Christos, and Pistis Sophia, I have come from the Light, from the place where the Light came into being, sat within itself, and appeared in the image of the Pleroma.

I am the Light's child, and I am the chosen of the living Father and Barbelo.

The evidence of the Father and Barbelo in me is movement, and meditation.

I go, then, in peace, and will tell no one what has happened within. In the name of the Nous, the Christos, and Pistis Sophia, Amen.

Blessing Ritual for a House

This ritual is especially beneficial when one has just moved house, after a serious illness or death, or in times of trouble. Materials needed: Consecrated water, salt, sage smudge or other 'cleansing' incense, icon or holy figure. All who live in the house should be present for the blessing.

The ritual begins inside the house at the entranceway.

Peace to this house and all who dwell within. ✠ Nous, Christos, Pistis Sophia. Amen.

When the Christos descended from the realms of the Aeons and came to dwell within the World of Forms, he made it into his house and shall keep his house with us. With water and fire, let us drive forth the influences of the Rulers of the World of Forms and invite the Christos and Sophia to dwell within this house in love, peace and gladness.

Light smudge and carry the icon/crucifix/holy image from room to room, and say the following prayers as each room is blessed with holy water and incense. Family members may be present and choose to participate by carrying incense/icon/etc.

Entranceways

Sprinkle consecrated salt before and behind the entrance.

In the name of the Christos and Sophia, let the Powers and Influences of the Archons quit this place and its residents forever!

We renounce your works, deeds and images, and the troubles resulting from your presence! May all who enter and exit this house, and all those who dwell within, do so in peace and harmony, and come to know the peace and benevolence of the Holy Spirit. Amen.

Living Room

In the name of the Christos and Sophia, bless this room that it may be filled with joy and happiness. Bless all those who visit this room, that they share in hospitality and friendship. Amen.

Dining Room

In the name of the Christos and Sophia, bless this room that all those who enter share in the nourishment of body and spirit. Let all those who enter this room be thankful for your many gifts and willing to share them with others. Amen.

Kitchen

In the name of the Christos and Sophia, bless this room and all who work herein. Let all who are hungry find refreshment with the Holy Spirit. Amen.

Bathrooms

In the name of the Christos and Sophia, let all who enter this room be cleansed in body, mind and spirit. Keep them in good health and protect them from harm. Amen.

Bedrooms

In the name of the Christos and Sophia, bless this room and all who sleep herein. Watch over them while they sleep, and deliver to them dreams of peace and joy that they may awaken refreshed and happy. Amen.

Other Rooms

In the name of the Christos and Sophia, bless this room and all who use it. Let the Holy Spirit abide here and watch over all who enter and leave. Amen.

Exterior

Circle the exterior of the house, stopping at the center of each quarter, where consecrated water is sprinkled and the Sign of the Cross is made with the smudge.

(At each stop) In the name of the Christos and Sophia, we cast all of the Powers and Influences of the Rulers out of the presence of this house and those who dwell within. Let all who near this house and depart this house enjoy the peace and benevolence granted by the Holy Spirit. Amen.

After all four quarters have been blessed, return to common area inside the house. Each person present kisses the icon/crucifix/figure and it is placed in a position of honor to symbolize the protection of the Pleroma. A candle may also be lit before it.

Let all who dwell within this house strive to keep it a place of happiness and light. Let them forgive those who have wronged them, and relax into the embrace of the Holy Spirit, in which this house and its dwellers now rest. Let us pray.

Unknown Mystery who dwells above the Pleroma, we honor your holy names. May your Aeons unfold over the World, and may your work be accomplished within the World as it is accomplished in the Pleroma. Provide us with the nourishment we require, and forgive us our imperfections as we try to forgive those who do us harm. Help us achieve the gnosis of the Light, and keep us safe from the clutches of the Archon, now and forever. Amen.

May the peace of the Father, Barbelo, the Christos and Sophia be with you and guide you always. ✢ Nous, Christos, Pistis Sophia.

Ritual of Self-healing and Laying-on of Hands

One of the most prevalent aspects of Jesus's ministry was the healing of the sick by the laying on of hands **This ritual is not intended as a substitute for professional medical care, but as a supplement thereto.** *One should always defer to professional physicians regarding treatment of the sick.*

Materials necessary: clean linen, consecrated water, oil, wine, bread and ash.

The sick room should be as clean as possible. Family and close friends are allowed in the room provided they are willing to participate in the ceremony.

Weather permitting, the windows should be open to allow fresh air into the room, and as much natural light as possible.

In the name of the Nous, Christos, Pistis Sophia, Amen. ✢

Sprinkle the room with consecrated water.

Peace be to this house and all who dwell within.

We dwell within the realms of imperfection and have been given imperfect bodies, susceptible to disease and sickness. The Christos, however, the truest and gentlest of all physicians, has also given us the power and ability to heal the body and the mind when beset by imbalances and illnesses.

I have been beset by (*name your illness or complaint.*)

The following has been stamped upon your soul, and in the presence of the Christos and Sophia, I wish to unburden myself this day.

In case the illness has psychological roots, the sick person should confess any errors or evil influences that may beset him or her. This may be spoken aloud or in silence, and one should feel free to clear the room of its occupants and allow the sick person a moment of privacy. Then, over oneself:

In the names of the Most Holy Christos and Sophia. Before me Armozel, Behind me Davethai, to my Left, Oriel, to my Right Eleleth. O you Four Luminaries who are Light above all Lights, be with me and protect me from all of the workings of the Archons that beset me! ⚨ Amen, Amen, Amen, Amen!

Taking consecrated oil, anoint yourself on the eyelids, ears, nostrils, lips, hands and feet, saying the following each time:

With this seal ⚨ I call upon the power of the Comforter. In the name of the Christos and Sophia, may I be healed and protected against the influence and presence of all of the Archons who would do me harm of body or spirit. Amen.

Unknown Mystery who dwells above the Pleroma, we honor your holy names. May your Aeons unfold over the World, and may your work be accomplished within the World as it is accomplished in the Pleroma. Provide us with the nourishment we require, and forgive us our imperfections as we try to forgive those who do us harm. Help us achieve the gnosis of the Light, and keep us safe from the clutches of the Archon, now and forever. Amen.

Jesus Christ and Holy Sophia, I pray for your gracious presence and power as you heal my sickness. In the name of the Christos and Sophia. ✚ In the sheep-pool in Soloam—its name in Hebrew is Bethsaida—the lord was found , in the Portico of Solomon the master was found. He healed the person who was bedridden by means of the Logos, and he opened the blind man's eyes. Hence I also, along with the archangels and the bodiless Aeons, shout and call out and say, Holy is God, whom the Aeons praise and the Angels revere.

Holy, mighty is he, whom the chorus of bodiless Aeons glorifies. Holy, immortal is he, who was revealed in the manger of the animals. Heal and make well the body of your servant N. ✚Nous, Christos, Pistis Sophia, Amen.

At this time, you should assess your primary concern. Is it pain? Fever? Chills? In what part of the body do the symptoms present? You should then consult the Tables found in Appendix III and create a mantra consisting of the names of the Archons listed using the following formula

Soul Ruler+Aspect Ruler+Active Ruler+Passive Ruler+Active Body Ruler+Passive Body Ruler

Example: If the sick person has chills and a deep cough in the lungs, we would compose the following mantra

Sabbaoth (Blood Ruler for Lungs)
Oroorrothos (Ruler of Cold for Chills)
Sabaoth (Blood Active Ruler)
Aarmouriam (Blood Passive Ruler)
Bano (Ruler of Lungs)

When this has been composed, anoint your eyelids with consecrated ash, saying:

As he passed by, he saw a man blind from birth. And his disciples asked him, "Rabbi, who sinned, this man or his parents, that he was born blind?" Jesus answered, "It was not that this man sinned, or his parents, but that the works of God might be displayed in him. We must work the works of him who sent me while it is day; night is coming, when no one can work. As long as I am in the world, I am the light of the world." Having said these things, he spat on the ground and made mud with the saliva. Then he anointed the man's eyes with the mud and said to him, "Go, wash in the pool of Siloam." So he went and washed and came back seeing. (John 9:1-7)

I call upon the names of the Powers which afflict me, according to the Apostle John's Secret Book.

Repeat the Mantra nine times.

You powers which afflict me, in the name of the Christos and Sophia I command you to heal my, that my soul and spirit, mind and heart may be refreshed. ✠Nous, Christos, Pistis Sophia, Amen.

With the clean linen, wash off the ashes and oil.

I invoke you, Almighty God, who is above every Ruler and Archon and Aeon and everything that has been named, who is enthroned above the Pleroma before you, through our Lord Jesus Christ and Lady Sophia, the beloved Mother and Child. Send out to me, Lord, your luminaries, who stand opposite your altar and are appointed for your holy services, Armozel, Oriel, Daveithai, Eleleth. Let them accompany me during all hours of day and night, and grant me victories, favor, good luck, success with all people small and great who I may encounter, during all hours of day and night.

For I have before me Jesus Christ and Sophia, who attend me and accompany me; behind me Yao Sabaoth; on my right and left the God of Abraham, Isaac and Joseph; over my face and heart Armozel, Oriel, Davethai, Eleleth. Protect me from every archon, male or female, and from every stratagem and from every name, for I am sheltered under the wings of Sophia.

O Jesus Christ, king of all the Aeons, almighty, inexpressible one, nurturer, master, almighty, noble child, kindly son, unutterable and inexpressible name, true form, unseen forever and ever. ✢Nous, Christos, Pistis Sophia, Amen.

I now partake of the Holy Eucharist, that I may be refreshed in body and in spirit.

Take a bite of the bread, and sip of the wine.

Now that I have partaken in the Mystery of the Eucharist, I give thanks to the Limitless Light for the manifestation of the Fullness within this world of Limitations.

I give thanks to you, O Limitless Light, who, through the mediation of the Most Holy Christos and Sophia have manifested the Glory of the Pleroma. I pray for the continued unfolding of the Fullness within the world of imperfection, and thank you for the blessed gifts which I have received.

I now go hence from this place and will wash in clean water, will eat and drink what is good and wholesome for my body, and will pray to the Christos and Sophia for my own health and that of all so afflicted. ✢ Nous, Christos, Pistis Sophia. Amen.

The rite concluded, you may wish to construct a healing sigil or phylactery. After you have recovered, you should return and bless the sickroom/house.

Sacrament of Reconciliation or Confession

This rite is offered for those who find value in the confession of errors.

The Scriptures say, "Now it is fitting that the soul regenerates herself and become again as she formerly was. The soul then moves of her own accord. And she received the divine nature from the father for her rejuvenation, so that she might be restored to the place where originally she had been. This is the resurrection that is from the dead. This is the ransom from captivity. This is the upward journey of ascent to heaven. This is the way of ascent to the father." (NHL)

The Lord be in my heart and upon my lips that I may truly and humbly share and release my error in the Name of the Father, and of the Son, and of the Holy Spirit our Mother. Amen.

I confess to the Unknown God and the Holy Mother Barbelo that I have missed the mark by my own error in my thinking, words, and deed, in things done and left undone; especially _____. For these and all other sins which I cannot now remember, I am truly sorry. Our Lord Jesus Christ, who has left power to his community to pronounce release to all those who truly seek God's light leaving behind error, and by his authority committed to me, I announce my freedom from all my error: ✠ Nous, Christos, Pistis, Sophia, Amen.

The scriptures remind us, "Remember that you are a King's child; see whom You hast you have served in your slavery. Remember your glorious robe, your splendid mantle, remember..." (Hymn of the Pearl)

Thanks be to God-- I go in peace.

Mysteries Of The Gnostic Ascent

The Sequence of the Gnostic Ascent is based loosely on the cosmology from the Secret Book of John, a Sethian Gnostic work found in various codices including the Nag Hammadi cache. The Gnostic Ascent also offers a kind of Guided Meditation on the elements thereof. Although these prayers do not require repetition, a manual aid to prayer, or chaplet, will be helpful as a mnemonic device

The sequence consists of an "ascent" from the World of Forms up into the realms of the Limitless Light. As we speak each prayer, we encounter different Aeons in the Realms of Light, and gradually pass through a number of different manifestations of God through in series of Mysteries, which also include prayers and scriptures from other Gnostic texts. Attribution has been provided as needed.

This sequence is meant to be interactive; if you like it, and would like to try it, we encourage you to replace these 'default' passages and prayers with your own favorite, or even those of your own composition. We also encourage the individual Gnostic to consider this Prayer Sequence as valuable to individual practice as the Roman Catholic might consider the Prayer of the Rosary.

1. OPENING PRAYER: "FATHER, HEAR US"

We begin with "Father, Hear Us," a composite prayer from the Letter from Peter to Paul *and* The Dialogue of the Saviour. *While speaking this prayer, we speak from within the World of Forms, calling out to our Father, the Limitless Light.*

We call upon our Father in the same way that Jesus called upon Abba, or that Horus called upon Osiris. Ours is the prayer of the supplicant, the cry of the individual trapped within a universe she had no say in creating.

Our cries are full of fear – not the fear of punishment, or of eternal damnation, but the Fear the All feels upon being separated into infinite fragments. We feel abandoned, unworthy, alone, filled with an ineffable sadness.

And yet, at the same time, we ask the Father to hear us knowing that the Father will respond. He will receive us as he received Jesus. He will redeem us through the medium of the Holy Sophia, our ever-radiant and resplendent Mother. And, as we cry to Him, even though we cannot see Him, we know his presence within the Pleroma and look forward to joining the ranks of the elect.

Father, Hear Us

Father, Father, Father of the light, who possesses the
incorruptions, hear us just as you have taken pleasure in your
holy child Jesus Christ.
For he became for us an illuminator in the darkness.
Yes, hear us!
Hear us, Father, just as you heard your only-begotten son,
and received him,
and gave him rest from any imperfection.
You are the one whose power is perfect;
your armor, resplendent, is full of the light above all lights;
your living presence touches the Pleroma;
the Word saves the Cosmos through the repentance of
Sophia;
life has come into existence because of you.
You are the thinking and the entire serenity of the solitary.
Again: Hear us just as you heard your elect.
Through your sacrifice, these will enter;
through their good works, these have saved their souls from
these blind limbs,
so that they might exist eternally.
Amen.

2. PRAYER TO THE LOGOS AND SOPHIA, REPUDIATION OF THE ARCHONS

Our opening prayer complete, our intention announced and our request for divine assistance made, we appeal to the Logos and Sophia, those saviours who descend into the limitations of matter on the rope-ladder of gnosis and save us, lifting us past the Archons, the false rulers of this world of forms. As we rise past the Archons, we repudiate them and their works.

The Logos, "Word," is the manifestation of the Christos, the Divine Autogenes (self-generated) who resided within Jesus Christ and delivered the living information to the realms of imperfection. Sophia, Wisdom, our divine Mother, is the feminine aspect of God, the Holy Spirit, The Comforter called the Paraklete. Word and Wisdom take us by the hands and lift us through the walls of the Black Iron Prison into the domain of the Archons.

The Archons are the rulers of the World of Forms, and are ruled by the Demiurge, their King, Yaltabaoth. The Secret Book of John *describes the Archons as follow:*

> *The name of the first one is Athoth, whom the generations call the reaper. The second one is Harmas, who is the eye of envy. The third one is Kalila-Oumbri. The fourth one is Yabel. The fifth one is Adonaiou, who is called Sabaoth. The sixth one is Cain, whom the generations of men call the sun. The seventh is Abel. The eighth is Abrisene. The ninth is Yobel. The tenth is Armoupieel. The eleventh is Melceir-Adonein. The twelfth is Belias, it is he who is over the depth of Hades.*
>
> *And he placed seven kings - each corresponding to the firmaments of heaven - over the seven heavens, and five over the depth of the abyss, that they may reign.*

. . . And the archons created seven powers for themselves, and the powers created for themselves six angels for each one until they became 365 angels. And these are the bodies belonging with the name the first is Athoth, a he has a sheep's face; the second is Eloaiou, he has a donkey's face; the third is Astaphaios, he has a hyena's face; the fourth is Yao, he has a serpent's face with seven heads; the fifth is Sabaoth, he has a dragon's face; the sixth is Adonin, he had a monkey's face; the seventh is Sabbede, he has a shining fire-face. This is the sevenness of the week.

But Yaltabaoth had a multitude of faces, more than all of them, so that he could put a face before all of them, according to his desire, when he is in the midst of seraphs.

As we rise past the Archons, we encounter their monstrous visages; they hiss and gnash their teeth, but when they hear our repudiation, which contains an admonition from the Gnostic book The Books of the Saviour or Pistis Sophia, and see the Logos and Sophia lifting us past their realms, they wail and moan grievously. Terrified, they cower and tremble at the majesty of the Logos and Sophia, and remove themselves allowing us to pass.

Prayer to the Logos and Sophia

Glory, Glory, Glory to You,
O Iesus Christos Parakletos Sophia,
Who was sent to redeem us,
O you who descended into the World of Forms,
You ineffable Word and Wisdom,
Forgive us our transgressions,
Free us from the chains of limitation,
And carry us to the Fullness of the Limitless Light.
Amen.

Renunciation of the Archons

Rulers of the World of Forms, hear me:
You usurpers of the rightful realm of perfection
I renounce you and your works, deeds, images.
Take your destiny!
I come not to your regions from this moment onwards.
I have become a stranger unto you for ever,
being about to go unto the region of my inheritance.
Rulers of the World of Forms, hear me:
I renounce you and your servants,
And commend my whole self to the Realms of Truth,
Now and forever.
Amen, Amen, Amen.

3. THE MYSTERIES OF THE FOUR LUMINARIES

We now enter the realms of the Mysteries of the Four Luminaries, emanations of God through which we ascend. The Word lifts us into Wisdom, Sophia, in Eleleth, the first of the emanations of the Luminaries we encounter after having renounced the Archons. Each Luminary possesses three qualities on which we must meditate before passing to the next Mystery. The qualities are represented by passages from Gnostic Scripture.

We pause within the realm of each Luminary and meditate on their mysteries. These passages from scripture can be replaced with personal favorites, and meditated upon for as long as one feels necessary. When we have completed our meditations upon the Mysteries, we hail the Luminary by name and title, and pass through to the next.

**Fourth Mystery of the Fourth Luminary, Eleleth:
Sophia (Wisdom):**

Wisdom summons you in her goodness, saying, "Come to Me, all of you, O foolish ones, that you may receive a gift, the understanding which is good and excellent. I am giving to you a high-priestly garment which is woven from every (kind of) wisdom."

The Teachings of Silvanus

Third Mystery of the Fourth Luminary, Eleleth:
Peace:

Jesus say "If two make peace with one another in one and the same house, they will say to the mountain: 'Move away,' and it will move away."

The Gospel of Thomas

Second Mystery of the Fourth Luminary, Eleleth: Perfection:

Since the perfection of the All is in the Father, it is necessary for the All to ascend to him.

The Gospel of Truth

First Mystery of the Fourth Luminary, Eleleth:

Holy are You, Holy are You, Holy are You, commander-in-chief, Eleleth, for ever and ever. Amen. I am king! Who belongs to Chaos and who belongs to the underworld?

Melchizedek, Trimorphic Protennoia

**Fourth Mystery of the Third Luminary, Daveithai:
Idea**

It is by virtue of his will that the Father, the one who is
exalted, is known, that is, (by virtue of) the spirit which
breathes in the Totalities and it gives them an idea of seeking
after the unknown one, just as one is drawn   by a pleasant
aroma to search for the thing from which the aroma arises,
since the aroma of the Father surpasses these ordinary ones.

The Tripartite Tractate

Third Mystery of the Third Luminary, Daveithai: Love:

Faith receives, love gives. No one will be able to receive without faith. No one will be able to give without love. Because of this, in order that we may indeed receive, we believe, and in order that we may love, we give, since if one gives without love, he has no profit from what he has given.

The Gospel of Philip

Second Mystery of the Third Luminary, Daveithai: Understanding:

You cannot receive understanding unless you know first that you possess it. In everything there is again this sentence.

The Sentences of Sextus

First Mystery of the Third Luminary, Daveithai:

Holy are You, Holy are You, Holy are You, commander of the aeons, man-of-light, Daveithai, for ever and ever. Amen.

Melchizedek

Fourth Mystery of the Second Luminary, Oriael: Memory:

"And as long as I am with you, give heed to me, and obey me; but when I depart from you, remember me. And remember me because when I was with you, you did not know me."

The Secret Book of James

Third Mystery of the Second Luminary, Oriael: Perception:

Names given to the worldly are very deceptive, for they divert our thoughts from what is correct to what is incorrect. Thus one who hears the word "God" does not perceive what is correct, but perceives what is incorrect. So also with "the Father" and "the Son" and "the Holy Spirit" and "life" and "light" and "resurrection" and "the Church (Ekklesia)" and all the rest - people do not perceive what is correct but they perceive what is incorrect, unless they have come to know what is correct.

The Gospel of Philip

Second Mystery of the Second Luminary, Oriael: Conception:

It is impossible for anyone to conceive of him or think of him. Or can anyone approach there, toward the exalted one, toward the preexistent in the proper sense? But all the names conceived or spoken about him are presented in honor, as a trace of him, according to the ability of each one of those who glorify him.

The Tripartite Tractate

First Mystery of the Second Luminary, Oriael:

Holy are You, Holy are You, Holy are You, commander, luminary of the aeons, Oriael, for ever and ever, Amen.

Melchizedek

**Fourth Mystery of the First Luminary, Armozel:
Form:**

I was among those who are united in the friendship of friends forever, who neither know hostility at all, nor evil, but who are united by my Knowledge in word and peace which exists in perfection with everyone and in them all. And those who assumed the form of my type will assume the form of my word.

The Second Treatise of the Great Seth

Third Mystery of the First Luminary, Armozel: Truth:

Truth appeared; all its emanations recognized it. They actually greeted the Father with a power which is complete and which joins them with the Father. For each one loves truth because truth is the mouth of the Father.

The Gospel of Truth

Second Mystery of the First Luminary, Armozel:
Grace:

For the perfection is majestic. He is pure, immeasurable mind.
He is an aeon-giving aeon. He is life-giving life. He is a
blessedness-giving blessed one. He is knowledge-giving
knowledge. He is goodness-giving goodness. He is mercy and
redemption-giving mercy. He is grace-giving grace, not
because he possesses it, but because he gives the
immeasurable, incomprehensible light.

The Secret Book of John

First Mystery of the First Luminary, Armozel:

Holy are You, Holy are You, Holy are You, exalted light, first aeon, Armozel, for ever and ever, Amen.

Melchizedek

4. THE MYSTERIES OF THE SPACE BEFORE THE LIMITLESS LIGHT

After meditating on the Four Luminaries, we enter the Space Before the Limitless Light, dwelling place of the highest of the Aeons. Before us stands Christos Autogenes, the self-created Christ, the Great One who appears to us as the Logos below the realms of perfection. We come to a realization of his nature with a selection from The Secret Book of John and continue ever upwards.

**First Mystery of the Space Before the Limitless Light:
Christos Autogenes**

For because of the word, Christ the divine Autogenes created
everything. And the eternal life and his will and the mind and
the foreknowledge attended and glorified the invisible Spirit
and Barbelo, for whose sake they had come into being.

And the holy Spirit completed the divine Autogenes, his son,
together with Barbelo, that he may attend the mighty and
invisible, virginal Spirit as the divine Autogenes, the Christ
whom he had honored with a mighty voice. He came forth
through the forethought. And the invisible, virginal Spirit
placed the divine Autogenes of truth over everything. And he
subjected to him every authority, and the truth which is in
him, that he may know the All which had been called with a
name exalted above every name. For that name will be
mentioned to those who are worthy of it.

Praise be to You, Divine Autogenes! Shed your Glory upon us
as we ascend to the Realms of the Limitless Light.

To continue our ascent, we must shed our earthly aspects and robe ourselves in the qualities of the Pentad of the Aeons of the Father, those Aeons who direct the process of emanation. We pray to their aspects as those who stand before the Gateless Gate, and recognize that the pentad is truly a decade, as each quality is masculine and feminine, microcosmic and macrocosmic.

In many ways, we are become like the Goddess Inanna in Sumerian mythology, who had to shed her garments to descend into the underworld. In our case, we are instead accompanied by Sophia, and we robe ourselves in the qualities of the Light. At the point in the prayer where we see "N," we speak our true names firmly and with all of our will.

Second Mystery of the Space Before the Limitless Light: Prayer to the Pentad of the Aeons of the Father

O You great and glorious powers of the Aeons of the Father, Hear the humble prayer of your servant, N.
May I attain knowledge of the Limitless Light through the mediation of Forethought, that I may not fall victim to evil thoughts, and may bring the ideal to the realms of imperfection;
May I attain knowledge of the Limitless Light through the mediation of Foreknowledge, that I may not remain asleep, and may bring gnosis to the realms of imperfection;
May I attain knowledge of the Limitless Light through the mediation of Imperishability, that I may become perfect with You, and may bring perfection to the realms of imperfection.
May I attain knowledge of the Limitless Light through the mediation of Eternal Life, that I may not taste death, and bring life to the realms of imperfection.
May I attain knowledge of the Limitless Light through the mediation of Truth, that I may not be ignorant of the self and God, and bring truth to the realms of imperfection.
I glorify You and give thanks to You, great Powers of the Pentad of the Aeons of the Father. May I be found worthy to pass You and enter into the presence of the Limitless Light. Amen, Amen, Amen, Amen, Amen.

We now stand before Barbelo, the Divine Mother-Father, He/She to whom we pray when we pray to the Mother Goddess or the Divine Father. Barbelo is the First Emanation from the Limitless Light, and we must petition Barbelo for admittance past the Gateless Gate.

Our petition comes from the Trimorphic Protennoia, or First Thought in Three Forms. *Within the presence of Barbelo, clad in garments of the Pentad of the Aeons of the Father, we shed the last of our Worldly concerns and revel in the divine love of the Mother of All.*

First Mystery of the Space Before the Limitless Light: Prayer to Barbelo, the Divine Mother-Father

O Thought that dwells in the Light,
You movement that dwells in the All,
She in whom the All takes its stand,
First-born among those who came to be,
        She who exists before the All.

You Protennoia, called by three names though dwelling alone,
You who are invisible within the Thought of the Invisible One,
Who is revealed in the immeasurable, ineffable.

You incomprehensible Mother-Father,
Dwelling in the incomprehensible.

You who move in every creature,
Hear the prayer of your humble servant.

I have been lifted to You through the medium of the Logos
and Sophia.

I have renounced the Archon and all of his works and deeds.

I have transversed the realms of the Four Luminaries,
Eleleth, Daveithai, Oriael, Armozel,
and have been completed in their completenesses.

I have stood in the presence of the Christos Autogenes,
and I have been robed in the glories of the Pentad of the
Aeons of the Father.

I pray You, o Mother-Father,

You who put on Jesus, bore him from the cursed wood,
and established him in the dwelling places of his Father.

I do not watch over their dwelling place;
I recognize you.

You, who are unrestrainable, together with your seed;
I pray You, place this humble spirit into the holy Light,
within an incomprehensible Silence
in which the self is no more, Amen.

5. THE MYSTERY OF THE LIMITLESS LIGHT

Finally we enter the Realm of the Limitless Light, which we cannot expound upon in the positive. After recognizing the paradoxical nature of this Realm with a negative description given in The Tripartite Tractate, *we meditate in Silence before the Perfection of the All.*

The Mystery of The Limitless Light

The form of the formless,
the body of the bodiless,
the face of the invisible,
the word of the unutterable,
the mind of the inconceivable,
the fountain which flowed from him,
the root of those who are planted,
and the god of those who exist,
the light of those whom he illumines,
the love of those whom he loved,
the providence of those for whom he providentially cares,
the wisdom of those whom he made wise,
the power of those to whom he gives power,
the assembly of those whom he assembles to him,
the revelation of the things which are sought after,
the eye of those who see,
the breath of those who breathe,
the life of those who live,
the unity of those who are mixed with the Totalities.

silence . . . .

6. PRAYER OF RETURN

After an indeterminate amount of timeless time within the presence of the Limitless Light, we descend back into the World of Forms. As we descend past the various Aeons, we acknowledge, thank, and bless them, asking them to be with us and protect us in our day-to-day existence.

We rush past the Aeons and Archons in reverse sequence, calling out to them as we pass. Finally, we settle back within our bodies inside the World of Forms, safe and content in the knowledge of what we have experienced, what we are experiencing and what we will experience.

Prayer of Return:

Praise be to the Limitless Light!
Be with me, guide and protect me!
Praise be to Barbelo, the Mother-Father!
Be with me, guide and protect me!
Praise be to the Pentad of the Aeons of the Father!
Be with me, guide and protect me!
Praise be to Christos Autogenes!
Be with me, guide and protect me!
Praise be to Armozel, Grace, Truth and Form!
Be with me, guide and protect me!
Praise be to Oriael, Conception, Perception and Memory!
Be with me, guide and protect me!
Praise be to Daveithai, Understanding, Love and Idea!
Be with me, guide and protect me!
Praise be to Eleleth, Perfection, Peace and Wisdom!
Be with me, guide and protect me!
Love and Compassion to the Archons,
Blind rulers of the Cosmos,
May they find redemption and
The peace that passes all understanding!
Praise be to the Logos and Sophia, Beloved Saviours!
Be with me, guide and protect me,
Now and Forever,
Amen.

Appendix 1: A Gnostic Chaplet

A simple Gnostic chaplet, or bead counter for the Gnostic Ascent prayer sequence, can be created with the following material:

1. Two pieces of sturdy thread of string or leather or chain or what have you, of equal length;
2. Two end-pieces, which can be as simple as beads or small crosses (sans the body of Jesus, of course) , or could also be meaningful personal items;
3. Eight beads of assorted colors;
4. Five buttons or discs, also of assorted colors.

The holes in the beads and discs/buttons should be large enough for both lengths of thread.

To create the chaplet, insert one piece of thread through a bead which will represent the Prayer to the Logos and Sophia, and the other through a bead which represents the Renunciation of the Archons. Tie the two threads together to the initial end-piece, the black cross at the bottom of the example figure, which is used to represent the first prayer, Father, Hear Us.
Now string both threads through the following sequence of items, which represent the remaining prayers in sequence: disc, bead, disc, bead, disc, bead, disc, bead, bead, disc, bead. Finally, tie the other end-piece to the top of the chaplet and cut the loose ends of string.

From bottom to top, the sequence should be as follows:

1. End-piece One (Hear Us, Father)
2. Bead (Logos, Sophia) | Bead (Renunciation of the Archons)
3. Disc (Mysteries of Eleleth: Wisdom, Peace, Perfection)
4. Bead (Eleleth)
5. Disc (Mysteries of Daveithai: Idea, Love, Understanding)
6. Bead (Daveithai)
7. Disc (Mysteries of Oriael: Memory, Perception, Conception)
8. Bead (Oriael)
9. Disc (Mysteries of Armozel: Form, Truth, Grace)
10. Bead (Armozel)
11. Bead (Christos Autogenes)
12. Disc (Pentad of the Aeons of the Father)
13. Bead (Barbelo)
14. End-piece (Limitless Light)

One begins the sequence at the bottom, and as one prays, one moves up the chaplet to the Limitless Light, at which point one pauses for silent meditation. One then says the Prayer of Return, counting back down the sequence of beads and discs.

The characteristics and colors of the materials used to construct the chaplet are of little consequence, though one can certainly follow a color scheme if one so desires. I prefer to use the same color for the discs representing the Mysteries of the Four Luminaries and the beads representing the Luminaries themselves. If, however, you are making your own and have limited resources, feel free to use beads of the same color, buttons of different sizes for the discs, fishing wire for the threads, etc.

You may wish to make your chaplet portable and carry it with you in a small bag. You may also wish to add a strap or band to the top of the chaplet, so it can be worn on a belt or other item of clothing.

Appendix 2: Gnostic Ascent-- The Recurrent Mysteries

The manifested but imperfect Cosmos, woven upon the fabric of the Pleroma, seeks its own redemption through constant prayer to God. Every selfless act of compassion, every exhilarating expression of Love, every radiant sunset over the mountains, every interaction between humanity and the numinous through music or are, all of these things serve to offer praise and thanksgiving to the Limitless Light, a symphony of interaction between the World of Forms and the perfect realms above.

The prayers of the Cosmos and its inhabitants ascend through the Aeons to the Limitless Light, and receive its grace and glory, returning to the World of Forms in a constant redemptive process. This process instills gnosis within the Cosmos itself, as well as those sparks of the light which are imprisoned within the limitations of matter. Thus do the Aeons deliver the prayers of the lost to the Limitless Light on our behalf, and return the comfort of the Holy Spirit to the spaces of deficiency.

As we pray the Gnostic Ascent, we become one with this process, and work to grant gnosis and salvation to ourselves and to the entire Cosmos. We rise through the Pleroma and the Aeons, encounter the Limitless Light, and descend back into the World of Forms. As this is a constant process, when so inclined, the Ascent can be performed in a recurrent form, truncated for mantric purposes. The recurrent Mysteries are ideal for daily practice in the morning and evening. The form is also useful in situations where one's time may be limited. The Gnostic Chaplet becomes especially useful for counting the Recurrent Gnostic Ascent.

Gnostic Ascent Prayer: Recurrent (Short) Form

Rubrics and Chaplet	Prayer
1. Sign of the Cross on Forehead.	1. † Nous, Christos, Pistis, Sophia, Amen.
2. End Piece One	2. Father, hear us. Amen.
3. Bead One	3. Word and Wisdom save us. Amen.
4. Bead Two	4. Rulers of this World, abandon us. Amen.
5. Disc One	5. Wisdom, Peace, Perfection, be with us. Amen.
6. Bead Three	6. Holy are You, Luminous Eleleth, Amen.
7. Disc Two	7. Idea, Love, Understanding, be with us. Amen.
8. Bead Four	8. Holy are You, Luminous Daveithai, Amen.
9. Disc Three	9. Memory, Perception, Conception, be with us. Amen.
10. Bead Five	10. Holy are You, Luminous Oriael, Amen.
11. Disc Four	11. Form, Truth, Grace, be with us. Amen.
12. Bead Six	12. Holy are You, Luminous Armozel, Amen.
13. Bead Seven	13. Thanks be to You, Christos Autogenes, for whom all has been, is, and will be, unto the Aeons. Amen.
14. Disc Five	14. Forethought, Foreknowledge, Imperishability, Eternal Life, Truth, array us in your Robe of Glory. Amen.
15. Bead Eight	15. Holy Mother-Father Barbelo, we do not watch over our dwelling places; We recognize you. We pray You, place this humble spirit into the holy Light, within an incomprehensible Silence in which the self is no more. Amen.
16. End Piece Two	16. Silence

17. Prayer of Return: Count beads and discs in reverse order as prayer is intoned.	17. Praise be to the Limitless Light! Praise be to Barbelo, the Mother-Father! Praise be to the Pentad of the Aeons of the Father! Praise be to Christos Autogenes! Praise be to Armozel, Grace, Truth and Form! Praise be to Oriael, Conception, Perception and Memory! Praise be to Daveithai, Understanding, Love and Idea! Praise be to Eleleth, Perfection, Peace and Wisdom! Love and Compassion to the Archons, Blind rulers of the Cosmos! Praise be to the Logos and Sophia, Beloved Saviours! All you Aeons and Powers of the Light, Be with me, guide and protect me, Now and Forever, Amen.
18. Sign of the Cross on Forehead.	18. † Nous, Christos, Pistis, Sophia, Amen.

Appendix 3. Tables of Rulers of the Body for Healing Rites

The following tables were developed from the long version of the Secret Book of John, and may be used during the healing rite.

Table 1. Rulers of Souls, Passive Aspects, Active Aspects

Ruler	Soul	Passive Aspect	Active Aspect
Athoth	Bone	Zathoth	Michael
Eloaio	Sinew	Armas	Ouriel
Astraphaio	Flesh	Kalila	Asmenedas
Yao	Marrow	Jabel	Saphasatoel
Sabbaoth	Blood	Sabaoth	Aarmouriam
Adonein	Skin	Qayin	Richram
Sabbataeon	Hair	Havel	Amiorps

Table 2. Rulers of Heat
Ruler: Phloxopha

Section I	Active Aspect	Passive Aspect
Crown	Raphao	
Head	Diolimodraza	Abron
Brain	Megiggesstroeth	
R. Eye	Asterechmen	
L. Eye	Thaspomocham	
R. Ear	Yeronumos	
L. Ear	Bissoum	
Nose	Akiopeim	
Lips	Banen Ephroum	
Teeth	Amen	
Molars	Ibikan	

Section II	Active Aspect	Passive Aspect
Neck	Yammaeax	Adaban
Tonsils	Basiliasdeme	
Uvula	Achcha	

Vertebrae	Chaaman	
Throat	Dearcho	

Section III	Active Aspect	Passive Aspect
R. Shoulder	Yakoubib	Tebar
R. Shoulder Joint	Koade	
R. Elbow	Mniarchon	
R. Underarm	Abitrion	
R. Hand	Oudidi	Krys
R. Fingers	Lampno	Treneu
Fingernails	Kriman	

Section IV	Active Aspect	Passive Aspect
L. Shoulder	Verton	Pnoumis
L. Shoulder Joint	Odeaor	
L. Elbow		Berberit
L. Underarm		Evanthen
L. Hand	Arbao	Beluia
L. Fingers	Leekaphar	Balbel
Fingernails		Kriman

Section V	Active Aspect	Passive Aspect
Chest	Pisandraptes	
R. Breast	Barbar	Astrops
L. Breast	Imae	Barroph
R. Ribs	Asphixix	Arachethopi
L. Ribs	Synogchouta	Zabedo

Section VI	Active Aspect	Passive Aspect
Abdomen	Senaphim	
Stomach		Gesole
Heart		Agromauma
Lungs		Bano
Liver		Sostrapal
Spleen		Anesimalar
Intestines		Thopithro
Kidneys		Biblo
R. Kidney		Pserem

	Active Aspect	Passive Aspect
L. Kidney		Asaklas
Breath		Aatoimenpsephei
Belly	Arouph	Areche
Navel		Phthave
Section VII	**Active Aspect**	**Passive Aspect**
Flesh		Entholleia
Marrow		Abenlenarchei
Bones		Chnoumeninorin
Sinews		Roeror
Spine		Taphreo
Veins		Ipouspoboba
Arteries		Bineborin
Section VIII	**Active Aspect**	**Passive Aspect**
Womb	Sabalo	
Genitals	Bathinoth	Sorma
Penis		Tarepspth
Testicles		Eilo
Section IX	**Active Aspect**	**Passive Aspect**
R. Buttock		Bedouk
R. Thigh	Charcharb	Gorma
		Kaiochlabar
R. Hip		Barias
R. Knee	Choux	Ormaoth
R. Shin	Aroer	Knyx
R. Ankle	Aol	Achiel
R. Foot	Bastan	Phiouthrom
R. Toes	Archentechtha	Boabel
Toenails		Miamai
Section X	**Active Aspect**	**Passive Aspect**
L. Buttock		Arabeei
L. Thigh	Chthaon	
L. Hip		Phnouth
L. Knee	Charcha	Emenun
L. Shin	Toechtha	Tupelon
L. Ankle	Charaner	Phneme

L. Foot	Marephnounth	Trachoun
L. Toes	Abrana	Phikna
Toenails		Miamai
Root		Labernioum

Table 3. Rulers of Coldness
Ruler: Oroorrothos

Section I	Active Aspect	Passive Aspect
Crown		Oaphar
Head	Azardomiloid	Norba
Brain		Theortsseggigem
R. Eye		Nemcheretsa
L. Eye		Machomopsath
R. Ear		Somunorei
L. Ear		Moussib
Nose		Miepoika
Lips		Nenab Mourphe
Teeth		Nema
Molars		Nakibi

Section II	Active Aspect	Passive Aspect
Neck	Xaeammai	Nabada
Tonsils		Emedsailisab
Uvula		Achcha
Vertebrae		Namaach
Throat		Ochread

Section III	Active Aspect	Passive Aspect
R. Shoulder	Biboukai	Rabet
R. Shoulder Joint	Edaok	
R. Elbow		Nochraimn
R. Underarm		Noirtiba
R. Hand	Ididou	Syrk
R. Fingers	Onpmal	Uenert
Fingernails		Namirk

Section IV	Active Aspect	Passive Aspect
L. Shoulder	Notrev	Simoupn
L. Shoulder Joint	Roeado	

L. Elbow		Tirebreb
L. Underarm		Nethnave
L. Hand	Oabra	Aiuleb
L. Fingers	Raphakeel	Leblab
Fingernails		Namirk

Section V	Active Aspect	Passive Aspect
Chest	Septardansip	
R. Breast	Rabrab	Psortsa
L. Breast	Eami	Phorrab
R. Ribs	Xixiphsa	Ipothechara
L. Ribs	Atouchgonys	Odebaz

Section VI	Active Aspect	Passive Aspect
Abdomen	Miphanes	
Stomach		Eloseg
Heart		Amaumorga
Lungs		Onab
Liver		Lapartsos
Spleen		Ralamisena
Intestines		Orthipoth
Kidneys		Olbib
R. Kidney		Mereps
L. Kidney		Salkasa
Breath		Eiphepsnemiotaa
Belly	Phoura	Echera
Navel		Evathph

Section VII	Active Aspect	Passive Aspect
Flesh		Aeillothne
Marrow		Eichranelneba
Bones		Nironinemounch
Sinews		Roreor
Spine		Oerphat
Veins		Abobopsoupi
Arteries		Nirobrnib

Section VIII	Active Aspect	Passive Aspect
Womb	Olabas	
Genitals	Thonithab	Amros

Penis		Pthpserat
Testicles		Olie

Section IX	Active Aspect	Passive Aspect
R. Buttock		Koudeb
R. Thigh	Brachrach	Amrog
		Rabalchoiak
R. Hip		Sairab
R. Knee	Xouch	Thoamro
R. Shin	Reora	Xynk
R. Ankle	Loa	Leicha
R. Foot	Natsab	Morthouiph
R. Toes	Athchetnechra	Leboab
Toenails		Aimiam

Section X	Active Aspect	Passive Aspect
L. Buttock		Eiebara
L. Thigh	Noathch	
L. Hip		Thounph
L. Knee	Achrach	Nuneme
L. Shin	Athcheot	Noleput
L. Ankle	Renarach	Emenph
L. Foot	Thnounpheram	Nouchart
L. Toes	Anarba	Ankiph
Toenails		Aimiam
Root		Mouinrebal

Table 4. Rulers of Dryness
Ruler: Erimacho

Section I	Active Aspect	Passive Aspect
Crown		Aoraph
Head	Drazadiolimo	Ronab
Brain		Troethmegiggess
R. Eye		Menasterech
L. Eye		Chamthaspomo
R. Ear		Numosyero
L. Ear		Oumbiss
Nose		Peimakio
Lips		Roumeph Nenba

Teeth		Enma
Molars		Kanibi

Section II	Active Aspect	Passive Aspect
Neck	Maeaxiam	Banada
Tonsils		Demebasilias
Uvula		Chaach
Vertebrae		Manchaa
Throat		Chodear

Section III	Active Aspect	Passive Aspect
R. Shoulder	Bibyakou	Barte
R. Shoulder Joint	Adeko	
R. Elbow		Chonmniar
R. Underarm		Onabitri
R. Hand	Didiou	Iskr
R. Fingers	Nolamp	Neutre
Fingernails		Mankri

Section IV	Active Aspect	Passive Aspect
L. Shoulder	Tonver	Mispnou
L. Shoulder Joint	Orodea	
L. Elbow		Beritber
L. Underarm		Thenevan
L. Hand	Baoar	Uiabel
L. Fingers	Pharleeka	Belbal
Fingernails		Mankri

Section V	Active Aspect	Passive Aspect
Chest	Draptespisan	
R. Breast	Barbar	Tropsas
L. Breast	Aeim	Rophbar
R. Ribs	Ixixasph	Ethopiarach
L. Ribs	Choutasynog	Edozab

Section VI	Active Aspect	Passive Aspect
Abdomen	Phimsena	
Stomach		Solege
Heart		Maumaagro
Lungs		Noba
Liver		Rapalsost

Spleen		Malaranesi
Intestines		Pithrotho
Kidneys		Lobib
R. Kidney		Rempse
L. Kidney		Saklasa
Breath		Psepheiaatoimen
Belly	Pharou	Cheare
Navel		Thaveph

Section VII	Active Aspect	Passive Aspect
Flesh		Leiaenthol
Marrow		Archeiabenlen
Bones		Meninorinchnou
Sinews		Rorroe
Spine		Reotaph
Veins		Pobobaipous
Arteries		Borinbine

Section VIII	Active Aspect	Passive Aspect
Womb	Alosab	
Genitals	Nothbathi	Masor
Penis		Pspthtare
Testicles		Loei

Section IX	Active Aspect	Passive Aspect
R. Buttock		Doukbe
R. Thigh	Charbchar	Chlabarkaio
		Magor
R. Hip		Asbari
R. Knee	Ouxch	Othorma
R. Shin	Eraro	Ixkn
R. Ankle	Lao	Elachi
R. Foot	Tanbas	Thromphiou
R. Toes	Techthaarchen	Belboa
Toenails		Maimia

Section X	Active Aspect	Passive Aspect
L. Buttock		Beeiara
L. Thigh	Thaonch	
L. Hip		Outhphn

L. Knee	Chachar	Nuneme
L. Shin	Chthatoe	Lontupe
L. Ankle	Anerchar	Nemeph
L. Foot	Phnounthmare	Chountra
L. Toes	Anaabr	Naphik
Toenails		Maimia
Root		Nioumlaber

Table 5. Rulers of Wetness
Ruler: Athuro

Section I	Active Aspect	Passive Aspect
Crown		Phaora
Head	Omiloidazard	Banor
Brain		Sseggigemtheort
R. Eye		Cheretsanem
L. Eye		Omopsathmach
R. Ear		Oreisomun
L. Ear		Ssibmou
Nose		Iokameip
Lips		Phemour Abnen
Teeth		Amne
Molars		Ibinak
Section II	**Active Aspect**	**Passive Aspect**
Neck	Maixeaam	Adanab
Tonsils		Sailisabemed
Uvula		Chaach
Vertebrae		Aachnam
Throat		Readoch
Section III	**Active Aspect**	**Passive Aspect**
R. Shoulder	Oukaibib	Etrab
R. Shoulder Joint	Okeda	
R. Elbow		Rianmnoch
R. Underarm		Irtibano
R. Hand	Ouidid	Rksi
R. Fingers	Pmalon	Erteun
Fingernails		Irknam
Section IV	**Active Aspect**	**Passive Aspect**

L. Shoulder	Revnot	Oupnsim
L. Shoulder Joint	Aedoro	
L. Elbow		Rebtireb
L. Underarm		Naveneth
L. Hand	Raoab	Labaiu
L. Fingers	Akeelraph	Lableb
Fingernails		Irknam

Section V	Active Aspect	Passive Aspect
Chest	Nasipsetpard	
R. Breast	Rabrab	Sasport
L. Breast	Miea	Rabphor
R. Ribs	Phsaxixi	Charaipothe
L. Ribs	Gonisatouch	Bazode

Section VI	Active Aspect	Passive Aspect
Abdomen	Anesmiph	
Stomach		Egelos
Heart		Orgaamuam
Lungs		Abo
Liver		Tsoslapar
Spleen		Isenaralam
Intestines		Othorthip
Kidneys		Bibol
R. Kidney		Espmer
L. Kidney		Asalkas
Breath		Nemoitaaeipheps
Belly	Ouraph	Eraech
Navel		Phevath

Section VII	Active Aspect	Passive Aspect
Flesh		Lothneaiel
Marrow		Nelnebaiechar
Bones		Ounchnironinem
Sinews		Eorror
Spine		Phatoer
Veins		Soupiabobop
Arteries		Enibnirob

Section VIII	Active Aspect	Passive Aspect

Womb	Basola	
Genitals	Ithabthon	Rosam
Penis		Eratthpsp
Testicles		Ieol

Section IX	Active Aspect	Passive Aspect
R. Buttock		Ebkoud
R. Thigh	Rachbrach	Oiakrabalch
		Rogam
R. Hip		Irabsa
R. Knee	Chxou	Amrotho
R. Shin	Orare	Nkxi
R. Ankle	Oal	Ichale
R. Foot	Sabnat	Ouiphmorth
R. Toes	Nechraathchet	Aobleb
Toenails		Aimiam

Section X	Active Aspect	Passive Aspect
L. Buttock		Araieeb
L. Thigh	Chnoath	
L. Hip		Nphthou
L. Knee	Rachach	Emenun
L. Shin	Eotathch	Eputnol
L. Ankle	Rachrena	Phemen
L. Foot	Eramthnounph	Artnouch
L. Toes	Rbaana	Kiphan
Toenails		Aimiam
Root		Rebalmouin

Sources and Recommended Reading

Unless otherwise noted, quotes and passages contained within this text are from the following sources:

Betz, Hans Dieter, ed. *The Greek Magical Papyri in Translation, Including the Demotic Spells,* Vol. 1. University of Chicago Press, 2001. (Referenced in text as **PGM**)

James, M.R., ed./trans. *The New Testament Apocrypha,.* Vol. 1 and 2. Apocryphile Press, 2004. (Referenced in text as **NTA**)

Meyer, Marvin and Smith, Richard. *Ancient Christian Magic: Coptic Texts of Ritual Power.* Princeton University Press, 1994. (Referenced in text as **ACM**)

Robinson, James, ed. *The Nag Hammadi Library.* Harper and Row, 1988. (Referenced in text as **NHL**)

6055056R00090

Printed in Great Britain
by Amazon.co.uk, Ltd.,
Marston Gate.